FIX-IT DUCK

*D*uck drove into my life one morning, smashed into a rock
and ever since I haven't been able to get rid of him. Not
that I'd really want to.

What I've come to love about Duck is that he's so passionate.
There's always something he wants to be doing…until the next
thing comes along.

Since moving into his new house, he's been pestering me with
his passion for fixing things. The trouble is, when Duck starts
fixing things, the problems are only just beginning…

For Clare

This edition produced for The Book People Ltd., Hall Wood Avenue, Haydock, St. Helens, WA11 9UL

First published in hardback in Great Britain by HarperCollins Publishers Ltd in 2001
First published in paperback by Collins Picture Books in 2002

1 3 5 7 9 10 8 6 4 2
ISBN: 0-00-776984-9

Collins Picture Books is an imprint of the Children's Division, part of HarperCollins Publishers Ltd.
Text and illustrations copyright © Jez Alborough 2001
The author/illustrator asserts the moral right to be identified as the author/illustrator of the work.
A CIP catalogue record for this title is available from the British Library.
Visit our website at: www.harpercollinschildrensbooks.co.uk
Printed in Thailand

Jez Alborough

FIX-IT DUCK

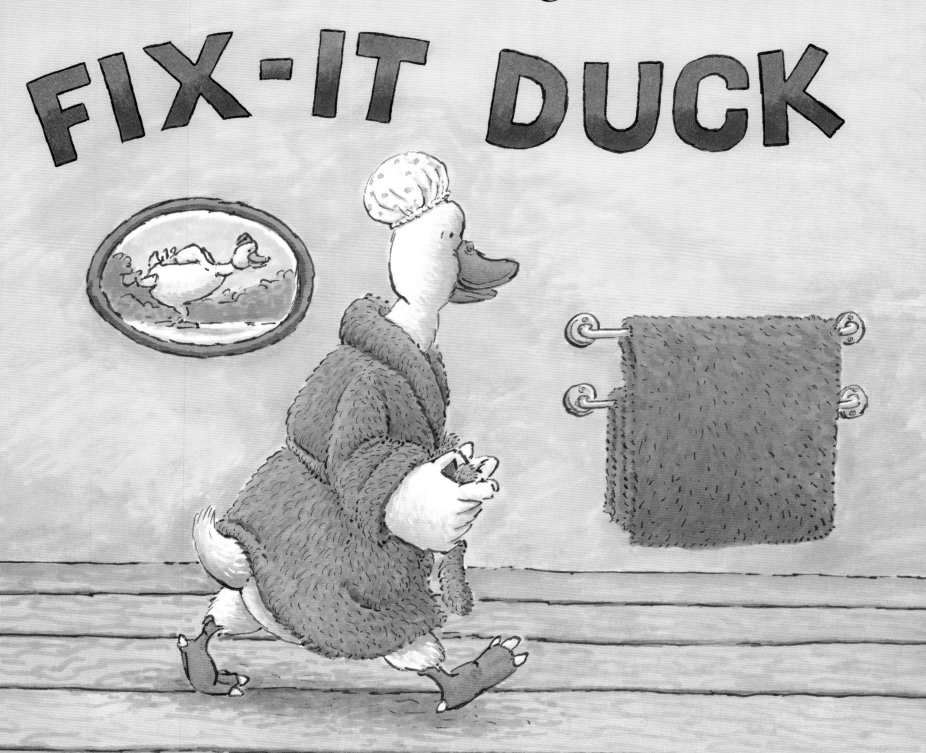

Plop! goes the drip that drops in the cup.
Duck looks down and Duck looks up.

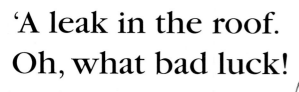

'A leak in the roof.
Oh, what bad luck!

This is a job for…

FIX-IT DUCK.'

He says, 'It's easy to repair.'
But how's he going to reach up there?

He can't climb up –
it's much too steep.

So he drives round to borrow

a ladder from Sheep.

Over the puddles
he hops and he skips

to Sheep's little house,
then, OOPS, he trips!

'Sheep!' calls Duck.
'It's only me.'

And he explains how the rain
had dripped in his tea.

When he reaches the part about fixing the leak,
they hear a rattle, creak and a squeak.

'It's my window,' says Sheep,
'it won't close, it's stuck.'

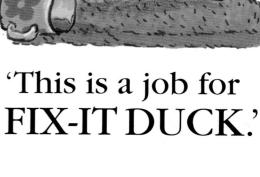

'This is a job for
FIX-IT DUCK.'

He does what he can to close up the gap.
He glues it, screws it and gives it a tap.

'The problem,' says Duck, 'is your glass is too thin.'
'My house,' wails Sheep. 'The rain's coming in!'

'What we need,' says Duck, with a glint in his eye,
'is to pull your house to somewhere dry.

Goat's got a shed. It can shelter inside.
Let's hook up your jeep and go for a ride.

Drive back slowly,
'til I say stop.'

Then all of a sudden,
something goes POP!

'A puncture,' says Duck. 'More bad luck.
We'll have to use my pick-up truck.'

But Sheep's little house won't join to the truck.

'This is a job for…   FIX-IT DUCK.'

'We're off,' says Duck as they speed down the track.

'Slow down on the bends,' calls Sheep from the back.

'Turn left,' he bleats as they skid round a curve.
'Hold tight,' comes the quack as the truck starts to swerve.

And the house should follow behind but instead…

...it unhooks from the truck

and rolls on straight ahead.

When Duck gets to Goat's he starts to explain
why they'd brought Sheep's house which was letting in rain.

'But where is it?' asks Goat.
Then as Duck turns to see,

Frog runs up shouting,
'It's following me!'

'Look up on the hill,'
gasps Goat in dismay.

'It's Sheep,' quacks Duck,
'and he's coming this way!'

'*Run!*' cries Frog.
'He's going to crash!'

'H - E - L - P !' bleats Sheep.

'It's broken,' says Duck. 'What a lot of bad luck.'

'Oh no!' moans Sheep '*not*…

FIX-IT

If only he hadn't come calling on me.
If only that rain hadn't dripped in his tea.'

DUCK!

'Not rain,' says Frog, with a shy little cough.

'He forgot to turn his bath tap off.'

THE
POP-UP
BOOK

THE POP-UP BOOK

Step-by-Step Instructions for Creating Over 100 Original Paper Projects

PAUL JACKSON

PHOTOGRAPHY BY PAUL FORRESTER

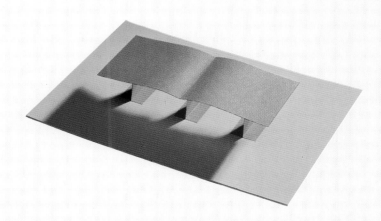

southwater

PUBLISHER'S NOTE

The publisher wishes to point out that the designs in this book
can all be made from thick paper or thin card (cardboard).
Cardboard has been given in brackets as the American
equivalent of the English term card. In addition, no occupation
is gentler than papercraft, but some general points should be
remembered:

▌ Craft knives, scissors, and cutting instruments should be used
with care.

▌ Always use a cutting board or mat to avoid damage to
household surfaces.

▌ While decorating papers, protect surfaces from paint, glue,
and varnish by laying down old newspapers.

This edition is published by Southwater

Southwater is an imprint of Anness Publishing Ltd
Hermes House, 88–89 Blackfriars Road, London SE1 8HA
tel. 020 7401 2077; fax 020 7633 9499
www.southwaterbooks.com; info@anness.com

© Anness Publishing Ltd 1993, 2003

This edition distributed in the UK by The Manning Partnership Ltd, 6 The Old Dairy, Melcombe Road, Bath BA2 3LR;
tel. 01225 478 444; fax 01225 478 440; sales@manning-partnership.co.uk
This edition distributed in the USA and Canada by National Book Network, 4720 Boston Way, Lanham, MD 20706;
tel. 301 459 3366; fax 301 459 1705; www.nbnbooks.com
This edition distributed in Australia by Pan Macmillan Australia, Level 18, St Martins Tower, 31 Market St, Sydney, NSW 2000;
tel. 1300 135 113; fax 1300 135 103; customer.service@macmillan.com.au
This edition distributed in New Zealand by The Five Mile Press [NZ] Ltd, PO Box 33–1071 Takapuna, Unit 11/101–111 Diana Drive,
Glenfield, Auckland 10; tel. [09] 444 4144; fax [09] 444 4518; fivemilenz@clear.net.nz

Project Editor Clare Nicholson
Designer Michael Morey
Photographer Paul Forrester
Illustrator John Hutchinson
Hand Model Paul Austin
Editorial Director Joanna Lorenz

Printed and bound in Singapore
1 3 5 7 9 10 8 6 4 2

Contents

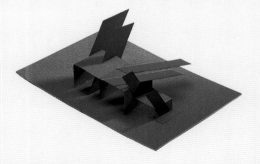

Introduction

....

This book is the first to explain basic pop-up techniques comprehensively, and to show how they have been used creatively by professional paper engineers, amateurs and students. It attempts to show that, although in the hands of a master a pop-up can be a remarkably sophisticated construction, the techniques themselves are delightfully simple and can be used creatively by anyone. The only requirements are a few easily learned hand skills and a little imagination – but then, that is no more than any art or craft requires.

Defining exactly what is, or is not, a pop-up is an awkward and perhaps pedantic exercise, but an important one. For the purposes of this book, a pop-up is a self-erecting, three-dimensional structure, formed by the action of opening a crease. This definition does not include rotating disks, lift-up flaps, pull tabs and other two-dimensional paper-engineered devices commonly, if mistakenly, described as pop-ups.

Whatever their exact definition, pop-ups are wonderful magical structures that confound our

BELOW
THE DOLL'S HOUSE
height 21 cm (8¾ in)
This elaborate pop-up made by Lothar Meggendorfer, is taken from a book published in the late nineteenth century. It collapses down to the size of an ordinary book. The pop-ups are made using the Scenery Flats technique, although some, such as the piano, were erected individually, by hand.

experiences of the physical world, in which two- and three-dimensions are rarely interchangeable. They have an appeal across all ages and cultures.

The first commercially available pop-ups were published in children's books in the middle of the nineteenth century, when London publishers Dean & Son and Darton & Co added three-dimensional effects to the by then familiar two-dimensional dissolving scenes and pull-tab effects. The books were immediate commercial successes.

Towards the end of the century, German publishers began to make and export a great number of pop-up books, and they found an eager market for their superb colour printing techniques, which were far in advance of what British publishers could achieve. Their success was made considerably greater by the paper engineering of Lothar Meggendörfer (1847–1925), whose contribution to the development of pop-up techniques is un-equalled. In more than a hundred books, many of which were translated and ran into numerous editions, he established the

potential of the technique, creating mechanisms that were extremely complex and full of character.

The political and economic problems in Europe during the early decades of the twentieth century meant that few pop-up books could be exported, or even sold domestically, so few were published during this time. Those that were published were mostly unimaginative and cheaply printed. However, in the late 1950s and 60s, colourful and technically innovative pop-up books were exported from Czechoslovakia, creating a huge revival of interest among paper engineers and publishers which continues to this day.

Since the 1970s, a great many pop-up books and greetings cards have been published. Paper engineers such as Wally Hunt in the USA, and Vic Duppa Whyte and Ron van der Meer in the UK, have been achieving ever more elaborate and ingenious effects, and are now familiar names to collectors of pop-ups.

I hope you will find this book easy to use and an inspiration. Pop-ups need not be difficult to make, but they do become tricky if you work too quickly, measure wrongly, and do not *think* your way through each stage of construction. Please work accurately and thoughtfully – your pop-ups will thank you!

Paul Jackson

Basics

· · · · · · · · · · · · · · · ·

How to Use the Book

The aim of *The Pop-up Book* is to enable you to master the techniques for constructing pop-ups and for designing your own pieces. Although you will not necessarily work through the book methodically, it is important that you read this chapter before starting out.

This chapter outlines the materials and equipment that you will need. These vary little from technique to technique, therefore lists of requirements are not given with each project. The chapter also demonstrates methods for cutting, folding and creasing, and diagrams

on page 16 illustrate the colour-coding system used throughout the book. These coloured symbols – green, red, brown and blue – are used in the step-by-step projects and in the diagrams, so that it is clear which lines are to be cut and which are to be folded. However, when making your own pop-ups you should always draw the design in faint pencil.

The first section of the book describes the techniques for constructing pop-ups. These are taught through sequences of step-by-step photographs and exercises for you to practise. The second section explains how to design pop-ups using

the skills that you have acquired. In most cases, the construction of the piece is not shown because the methods are the same as those used earlier. The techniques required for making each design are cross-referenced to the first section. It is, therefore, important that you have a good grounding in the techniques, even if you have not covered them all, before launching into design. If you find a design that you like, but which uses a method you have not learned, you will find it easier if you turn back to the first section and work through the relevant exercises before attempting something more ambitious.

on page 16 illustrate

OPPOSITE
J U N I
height 30 cm (12 in)
Juni is one of the twelve designs – one for each calendar month – produced as a set by Domberger, KG, a German printer. Each design is created by folding a single crease to make a sequence of criss-crossed shapes. The placement of the crease, and the shape of the free-standing forms, differ from month to month.

Papers and Cards

The choice of paper or card (cardboard) for a pop-up is important: if the paper is too thin, the pop-up will be weak and may collapse; if the card is too thick, the backing sheet will not close tightly shut around the pop-up inside. That said, there is a surprising margin for error and it is unnecessary to suggest precise weights or thicknesses. In general, try to use a sheet that will hold a crease well without cracking. This should not be a problem, as most papers and cards are manufactured to hold a crease, though some artists' papers such as watercolour paper do not, and should be used with discretion. It is better to use papers and cards that feel densely compacted rather than spongy or aerated.

It may be tempting to use the most inexpensive paper or card, but this is often a false economy. Inexpensive stock tends to turn brittle or yellow, or fades with age, sometimes distressingly quickly. This is because cheaper pulps are usually acidic and deteriorate by the natural process of oxidization (when the pulp comes into contact with the air). If you want your pop-ups to last for many years, check that the paper or card you use is described as "pH neutral", "acid free", or "permanent". It will be more expensive, but the extra cost will be more than compensated for by durability. However, any paper or card of reasonable quality will remain in good condition for some time, particularly if the pop-up is stored closed in a dark place.

A selection of papers and cards can be found at art and craft suppliers, and sometimes at stationers' or toy shops. Some cities have specialist retail suppliers, and paper merchants (not paper mills) are another source. All merchants will provide sample books called "swatches" free of charge, from which samples may be ordered. Often, they will supply a reasonable number of free sample sheets, particularly if delivering to a business address (it is worth a try).

Most merchants sell "designer pads" or "student pads" at cost price. They are exceptionally good value for money and contain several A3 sheets (approximately the size of this book when open) of each weight and colour in a particular range of papers and/or cards. Several pads from different ranges will last the most dedicated pop-up enthusiast many months, even years. The business pages of a telephone directory will contain details of local paper merchants.

For practice though, quantities of inexpensive papers are needed. The best source is photocopy (Xerox) paper, available from the quick print shops which are now found in most shopping centres. One thousand sheets of A4 (Letter Size) paper can be bought for about the same price as this book. Alternatively, computer paper and writing paper are good quality practice papers. If stiff card is needed, cut up cereal boxes, old LP covers and such like. In truth, it hardly matters what you practise with, as no one will see it.

Correct storage of paper and cards is important, and is often overlooked. Never leave large sheets rolled up for long periods, or they will not unroll

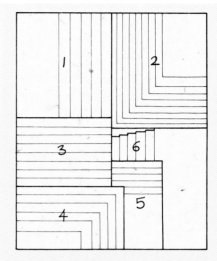

1 Marble-effect papers

2 Standard coloured papers, available in a wide range of shades

3 Embossed papers

4 Mottled papers

5 Deckle-edged rag papers, rough to the touch

6 Textured and embossed papers

later; never leave paper in strong sunlight, or it will fade; do not store it in a damp room, as the fibres will absorb moisture and warp the sheets; and never stuff an unrolled sheet into a drawer or cupboard where it will be damaged. Instead, keep the sheets flat inside an artist's portfolio, between large sheets of stiff card, or on the floor beneath a sofa or bed. Better still, invest in a plan chest. For the serious papercraft enthusiast, this is an essential investment. Good quality second-hand chests can be found at most office suppliers. If the storage of large sheets is a problem, cut them down to a more manageable size: pop-ups rarely need to be made from large pieces of paper.

Decorating Paper

It is not essential to decorate the paper and card (cardboard) used to make pop-ups. The play of light and shade over an undecorated surface can look beautiful, and clearly informs the eye about the structure of the piece. By contrast, an over-decorated surface can be confusing because the eye sees the two-dimensional decoration dominating the three-dimensional form, which creates the illusion of a flat surface. So, if you lack confidence in your drawing skills, or are unsure how to control pattern, colour and texture, or simply do not have decorating media to hand, leave your pop-ups plain – they will still look stunning, particularly if the papers and cards are of good quality.

If a pop-up *is* to be decorated, be careful when using water-based media. Water makes most papers and cards "cockle"; that is, warp and ripple. Not only does this look unsightly, but it makes a pop-up difficult to shut. So, use gouache, watercolour and poster paints with care, testing them out first. Even broad marker pens and felt-tipped pens can cockle paper. One solution is to use only those papers and cards designed to take water, such as watercolour paper.

Coloured pencils, pastels, charcoal and pens and pencils are much gentler and generally will not cockle paper, though they will need a good fixative (a cheap hair spray makes an inexpensive alternative to expensive artists' fixatives) to make them permanent. If a fixative is not used, pigment may transfer from the original surface to the one it is pressed against when the pop-up is closed, spoiling the surface design. Test for this before a final card is made.

There are other decorative techniques that can also be used, such as photographic collages, transfers, sticky paper shapes, glitter, fabric, gift-wrap paper, wallpaper and, indeed, anything else that comes to mind. The only practical considerations are that the finished pop-up should not be too thick to close flat, and that no glue should remain on the surface, or the two halves will stick together when the card is closed.

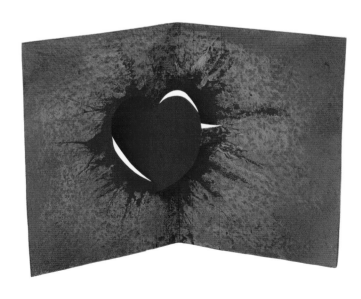

felt-tipped pens

coloured pencils

fixative

poster paints

crayons

marker pens

gouache paints

watercolour paints

pastels

Alizarin Crimson

Rose Doré

Indian Yellow

Cerulean Blue

How to Crease

The making of strong, accurately placed creases is essential for the construction of a successful pop-up. There are three main ways to form a crease. The choice of which method to use depends on what materials you use to make your pop-up.

By Hand

It is much harder than you would imagine to crease accurately by hand, therefore, hand creasing is suitable only for thin and medium-weight papers. Hand creasing thick paper or any card (cardboard) creates inaccurate creases and a rough edge along the fold.

Scoring

Scoring is only possible with thick papers and cards (cardboards). A sharp knife cuts partly through the sheet along the line of the crease, so that the sheet will fold more easily. The sheet must be scored on the **mountain** side of the crease (the outside of the fold). The crease will be sharp and straight, but care must be taken to score neither too deeply nor too shallowly. A little practice is helpful.

Though an easy technique, scoring weakens the card along the line of the crease because part of the thickness has been cut through, so it is not as strong as indenting.

Indenting

Whereas scoring breaks the surface of a sheet, indenting compresses the sheet along the line of the crease. The choice of tool for indenting is important. It must be neither too sharp (or the card will be scored) nor too blunt (as this will make the line of the crease too broad). A bookbinders' bonefolder is a good tool, as is a dry ballpoint pen, or even the handle of a scalpel. The tool must be run along a straight-edge and pushed hard into the card. Unlike a scored crease, which is made on the mountain side, an indented crease is made on the **valley** side (the inside of the crease).

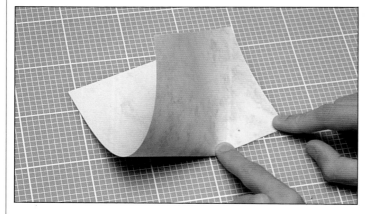

ABOVE LEFT Creasing by hand.

ABOVE RIGHT Scoring.

LEFT Indenting.

Equipment

The list of essential equipment is short, and most items can be bought cheaply from a local stationer's shop: pencils, ruler, compasses, protractor, cutting mat, scalpel and blades, craft knife and eraser. The self-healing cutting mat is an expensive item, but it will last for many years without becoming rutted. A thick cutting mat made from wood, or thick card (cardboard) will not stay smooth for long and will quickly begin to dull a cutting blade and send it off-line down a rut.

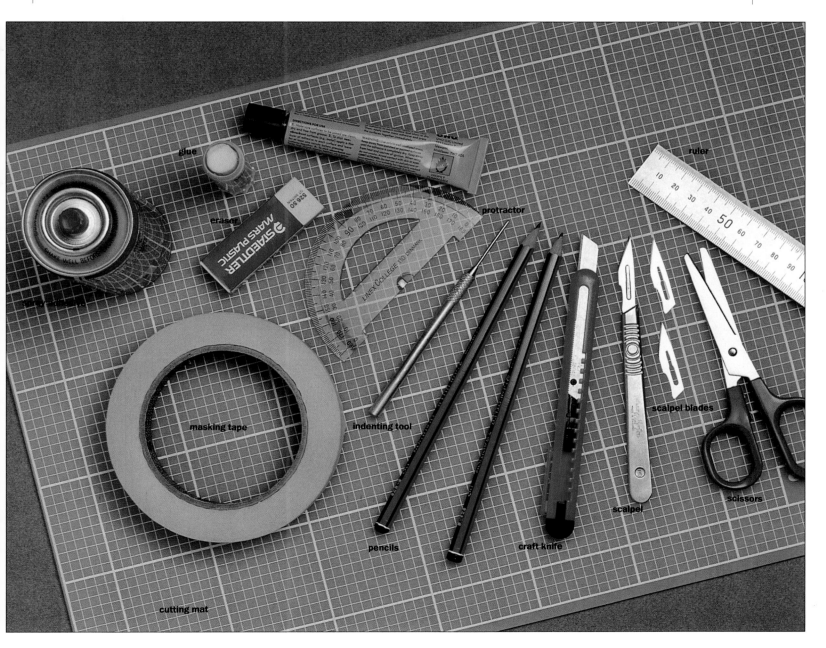

glue

ruler

eraser

protractor

masking tape

indenting tool

scalpel blades

pencils

craft knife

scalpel

scissors

cutting mat

Symbols and Terminology

The symbols used in the explanatory diagrams are similar to those used in origami books because they refer to the same processes of folding and unfolding. Other symbols are used here to describe cutting and gluing.

For clarity, the conventional origami dot-dash symbols for mountain and valley folds have been replaced by green lines for valleys (because valleys are green) and red lines for mountains. When working through the projects in the book, refer back to this page if you are unsure about a symbol.

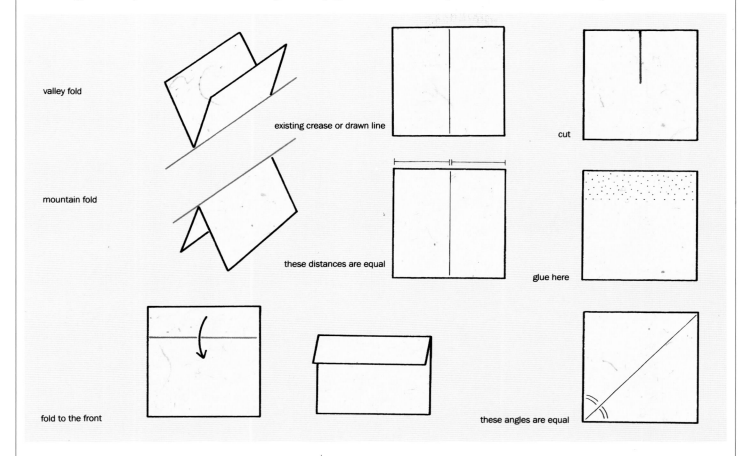

valley fold

existing crease or drawn line

cut

mountain fold

these distances are equal

glue here

fold to the front

these angles are equal

First, Make a Rough

The temptation for eager novices is to try constructing a finished pop-up without first making a rough. Unless the design is unusually simple and your understanding of its construction is complete, this approach will probably end in frustration.

Instead, use whatever rough paper and card (cardboard) is to hand and take a little time to make a practice pop-up. Every design will have its hidden subtleties and problems which are best understood before the final version is made. Strategies for overcoming any difficulties can then be developed while making the rough.

If the paper or card is to be decorated, practise techniques on part of the rough, preferably on the same kind of paper that will be used for the final pop-up. This will ensure that your chosen medium will not cockle the sheet if it is a water-based paint or solvent-based marker, and that it will hold fast if it is a dry pigment such as pastel.

How to make a Sturdy Backing Sheet

Throughout this book, the sheet of card (cardboard) that folds around the pop-up to protect it is called the backing sheet. If the pop-up is constructed from just one sheet (*see* One-piece Techniques, **page 21**), the backing sheet is integral.

For a pop-up in which the backing sheet opens flat (*see* Multi-piece Techniques, **page 69**), it is important that the sheet *does* open absolutely flat, so that the pop-up can assume its correct three-dimensional shape. The crease down the middle of the backing sheet is referred to as the gutter crease. A sheet of card that is scored or indented down the centre to create the gutter crease will not completely unfold to lie flat, so the crease must be made by other means. This is how:

1 Cut the card (cardboard) in half, down the line of the gutter crease.

2 Take one half of the card and run sticky tape along the back.

3 Cut the ends of the tape off at the top and bottom.

4 Take the other half of the card and place it on top, outside facing upwards, and fold the sticky tape over it.

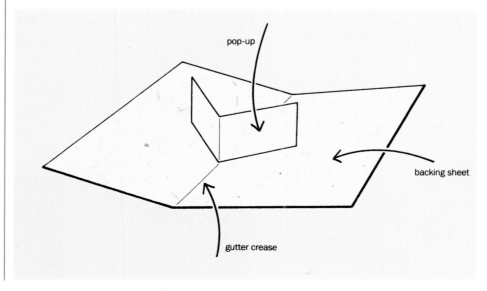

pop-up

backing sheet

gutter crease

5 The backing sheet is now complete.

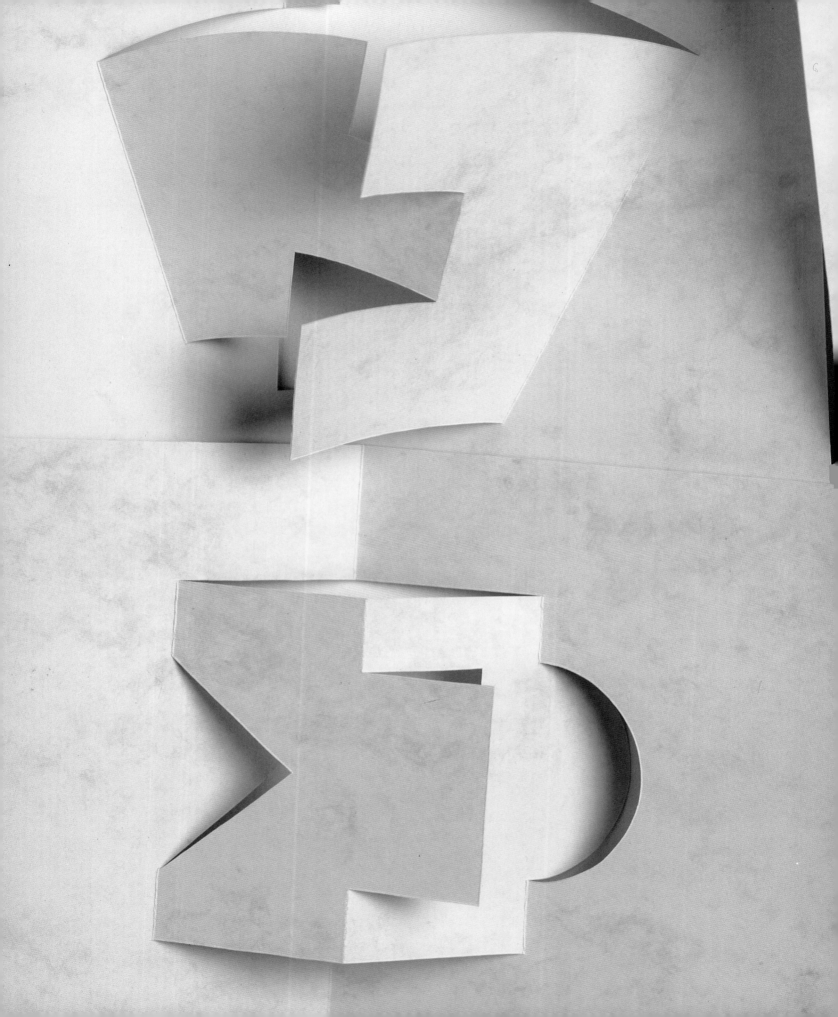

Techniques

··

This section covers all the main techniques for constructing pop-ups. It is divided into two chapters which cover one-piece techniques and multi-piece techniques. The aim of this section is to give you the confidence and knowledge to be able to go on to design your own pop-ups.

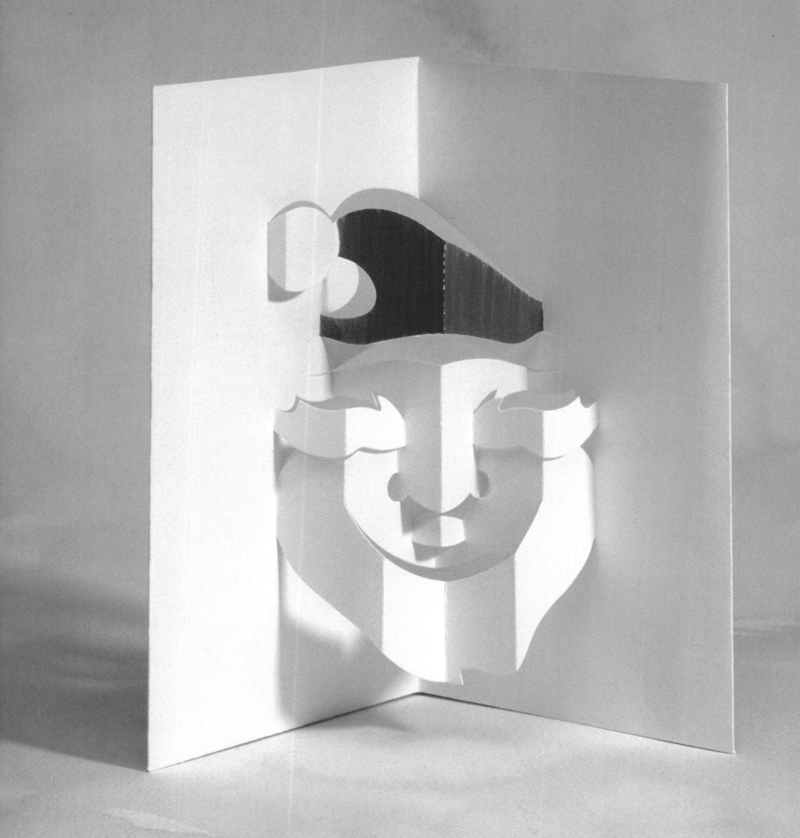

One-piece Techniques

There is something undeniably satisfying, even magical, about folding and cutting a single sheet into a recognizable form or beautiful abstract that is three-dimensional but which can collapse flat. Even a simple pop-up can look effective and will be appreciated by those who see it. It is not necessary to evolve complex designs, or to have a comprehensive understanding of the nuances of each technique before interesting designs can be made (though of course the greater your knowledge, the more technical options available to you).

One-piece pop-ups are in some ways the most basic to construct, yet in other ways they can be the most perplexing. The limitation of only using one sheet of paper imposes a constraint similar to that of origami, and demands a similarly creative approach. The evolution of a one-piece pop-up requires the ingenuity of a puzzle solver and the logic of an engineer This need not be as intimidating as it sounds: one-piece pop-ups are constructed in a very systematic way (they have to be, to fold flat).

Fortunately, all the techniques are simple to understand. And once understood, extraordinarily elaborate systems may be developed from them, particularly if some of the more open-ended techniques are used such as the Generations and Cut Aways. Before attempting to create your own more complex designs, you need to understand how to apply each technique and how one technique differs from another, and you need to have made some, or preferably all, of the examples. A little patience at this early stage will enable you to reap great rewards later.

Work through the techniques with care. At any stage, experimentation will give you a deeper understanding of what you have learned. Do not be discouraged by an early failure, because to remake something successfully will cement that technique in your mind.

OPPOSITE
FATHER CHRISTMAS
height 17 cm (6¾ in)
The careful cutting of the hat and facial features gives expression to what might have been a characterless design - when working within the constraints of geometric principles, the most difficult thing to achieve is character. The face is symmetrical, but the asymmetrical hat and its red colouring identify the subject.

Angle of Crease

Single Slit

. . . .

In a one-piece pop-up, the most elementary technique is that of the Single Slit. Nevertheless, from this very simple beginning an astonishing range of interesting forms can be made, providing the designer understands the variations of slit and crease that the technique can be put through, and how these can be combined.

In the Angle of Crease technique, the shape of the slit remains constant but the angle of the crease changes, creating a range of surprisingly different forms. First, work through the step-by-step example, then the variations that follow. In the first two variations, the shape of the slit remains the same as for the step-by-step example, but in the other three the slit is at 45 degrees to the gutter crease. In each case, the angle of the crease changes.

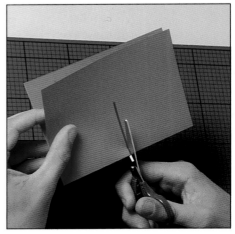

1 Fold a sheet of stiff paper in half. Measure along the folded edge (the gutter crease) and mark the halfway point. Using a pencil, draw a line from the crease into the middle of the paper. Cut along this line.

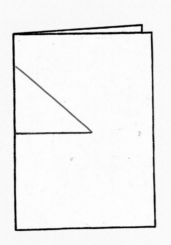

This diagram indicates the angle of crease and shape of slit formation for the step-by-step sequence.

5 This is the critical step. Pull up the triangle while also folding the paper shut again. All the creases must form simultaneously – they should appear as shown here. Note, there is only one mountain crease, down the middle of the triangle; the others are valleys.

2 Carefully fold along a line from the end of the slit to the gutter crease, creating a triangle. Press firmly.

3 Unfold the triangle so that it is in its previous position, then fold it to the back of the sheet, once again creasing firmly along the same line.

4 Unfold the triangle once again, then unfold the gutter crease, opening out the card completely.

6 Finally, close the pop-up and press it flat, strengthening all the creases.

RIGHT This configuration of mountain and valley creases in relation to the gutter crease and to the slit, will be seen many times throughout the book.

Angle of Crease Variations

LEFT: *I (LEFT)* and *II (RIGHT)* Despite the constant shape of the slit, the different angles of the crease will create different forms.

BELOW: *III (LEFT)*, *IV (CENTRE)* and *V (RIGHT)* Variation V, with its near horizontal crease, pivots a long way as the card is opened, whereas the other two remain more static when opened.

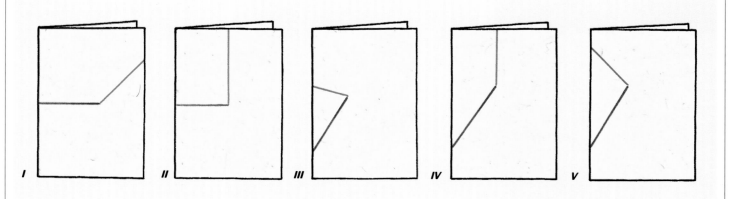

I   II   III   IV   V

FISH

height 30 cm (12 in)

The double "V" mouth made by using the Angle of Crease technique, animates the fish – as the card opens, the mouth closes. Torn paper creates the water effects. The off-centre depiction of the fish adds much visual interest to the pop-up.

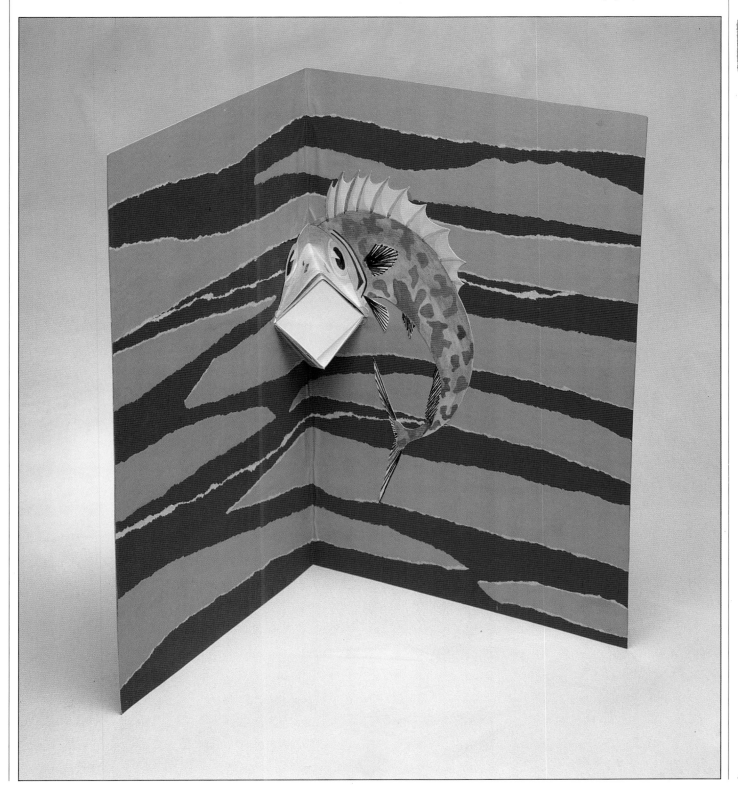

Shape of Slit

Not only can the angle of the crease change, as shown in the previous technique, but the shape of the slit itself can also change. When these two variables are used in combination, the range of possible forms becomes immense. Follow through the step-by-step sequence, and then make each of the variations to learn the full potential of this technique.

1 Having drawn the construction, use a craft knife to cut along the brown lines.

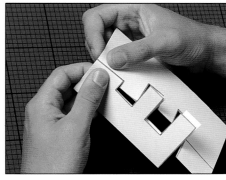

2 Fold along the two green lines, one at the top and the other at the bottom, creating valley creases.

3 Open the pop-up, and re-crease the gutter crease as a mountain fold.

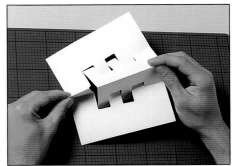

4 Similarly, re-crease the small step-shaped pop-up at the bottom of the paper (on the left of the picture) to create a mountain crease down this part of the gutter.

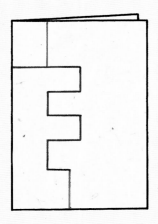

Fold a sheet of stiff paper in half, and draw the diagram shown above. (For clarity, coloured lines have been used in this example, but you should draw in pencil.)

RIGHT The arms of the pop-up pierce the plane of the backing sheet to create a structure that can be viewed from all sides.

O N E - P I E C E   T E C H N I Q U E S

DOVE

height 19 cm (7½ in)

This elegant pop-up design is achieved with remarkable simplicity: the angled creases between the wings and the tail tilt the dove away from the vertical cloud support. The curved outline of the cloud also extends around the dove to unite the two visually.

Shape of Slit Variations

RIGHT: *I (LEFT)* and *II (RIGHT)* and **BELOW:** *III (LEFT)*, *IV (CENTRE)* and *V (RIGHT)* These are just a few of the very many pop-up forms that can be made using this technique. A little time spent making these, and any other variations that come to mind, will quickly create a firm understanding of the basic cutting and creasing possibilities of one-piece pop-ups.

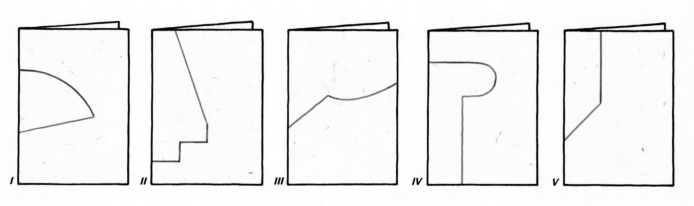

I *II* *III* *IV* *V*

Asymmetric Slit

The two variables explained in the previous projects, Angle of Crease and Shape of Slit, create forms that are symmetrical to the axis of the gutter crease. There is also a method of achieving asymmetric forms which will further expand your knowledge of Single Slit techniques.

1 Fold a sheet of stiff paper in half. Draw a straight line upwards on the diagonal from the gutter crease. (For clarity, coloured lines have been used in this example, but you should draw the design in pencil.)

2 Carefully fold the paper backwards along this line. Crease firmly.

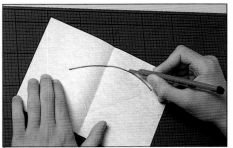

3 Unfold the paper, so that it is in its previous position, then fold it forwards along the same crease line.

4 Unfold the sheet of paper and open it out. This shows the completed preparatory crease pattern.

5 In pencil, draw a line of any shape that begins and ends on the "V" creases. Cut along this line using a craft knife.

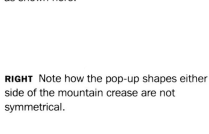

6 Form a central mountain fold by pulling the pop-up shape upwards while closing the card shut again – all the creases should be formed simultaneously. You will end up with one mountain crease and the rest as valleys, as shown here.

RIGHT Note how the pop-up shapes either side of the mountain crease are not symmetrical.

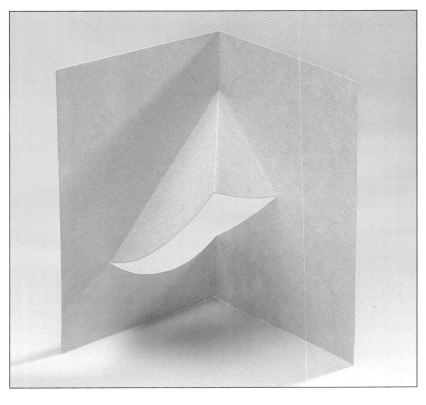

PIRATE DUCKS
height 11 cm (4¼ in)
This whimsical card shows how, with the skilful use of a complex cut silhouette and added artwork, a narrative scene may be devised which, though elaborate, is made from a simple pop-up technique – the Asymmetric Slit. Coloured pencil has been added to a photocopied drawing, reproduced on conventional photocopy paper, and given strength by being folded as a double layer.

Asymmetric Slit Variations

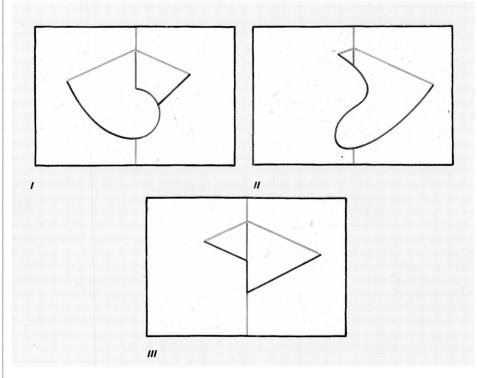

I

II

III

BELOW: *I (LEFT)* This pop-up is similar to variation II but it makes maximum use of the overhanging card. *II (CENTRE)* Note how the gutter crease does not form down the bottom part of the pop-up. To achieve this, it is necessary to draw the entire construction on an uncreased sheet, then to crease and slit only where essential. *III (RIGHT)* In this example, part of the slit has been formed in line with the gutter.

Asymmetric Angles

This technique creates a curious perspective effect. It is essential that the entire construction is accurately drawn before any creases are made. You will need a protractor to ensure that the angles are exactly in line with each other.

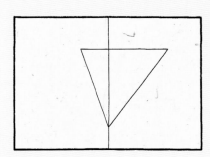

Using a pencil, draw the gutter crease (but do not crease it) and mark a focal point somewhere on this line. Then draw a horizontal line extending further to the right of the gutter crease than the left. Join up the horizontal line with the focal point to create triangles of unequal size either side of the gutter crease.

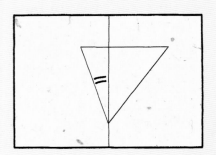

Using the protractor, measure the angle between the gutter crease and the left-hand diagonal line.

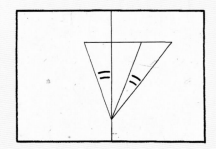

Reproduce the same angle on the inside of the right-hand diagonal line. Draw a line to mark this angle.

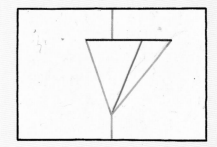

Finally, erase the central section of the gutter crease from the construction. (For clarity, coloured lines have been used in this diagram to show which lines are for folding and which are for cutting.)

1 Having carefully drawn the construction, cut along the brown line.

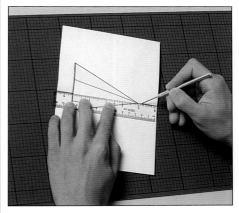

2 Indent or score the crease lines. Do not crease them by eye, as this will not be sufficiently accurate.

3 Begin to form the pop-up by creasing the red lines as mountain folds and the green lines as valley folds.

4 It is often easier to strengthen the creases by working from the back.

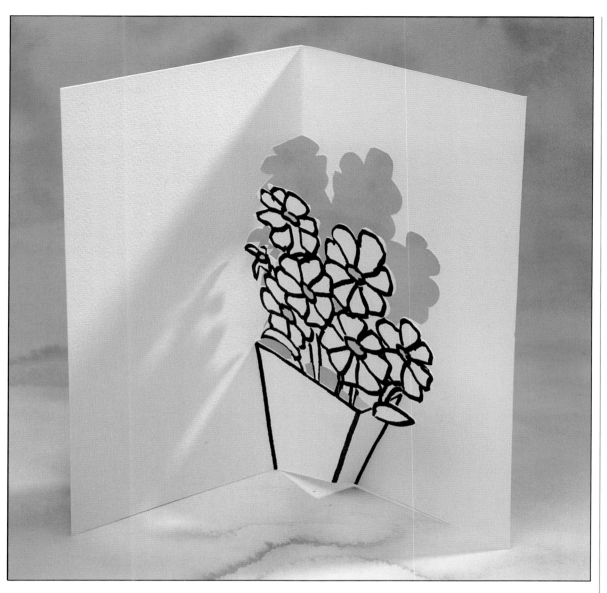

VASE OF FLOWERS
height
19 cm (7½ in)
The curious perspective created by the Asymmetric Angles technique adds greatly to an otherwise conventional pop-up. The use of black outlines, minimal touches of yellow and a heavily textured card (cardboard) creates a strong graphite-like effect.

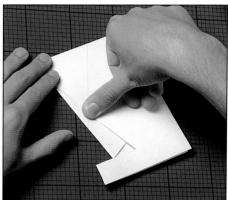

5 Flatten the pop-up and press it firmly to
.. reinforce the creases.

RIGHT Note that one triangular face of the pop-up is larger than the other, and that unlike previous techniques the mountain crease is not in line with the gutter crease.

Asymmetric Angles Variations

I (LEFT) Two asymmetric pop-ups are made from the one slit. Note that neither pop-up extends along the full length of the slit. *II (CENTRE)* In this design the focal point is located beyond the area of the backing sheet. *III (RIGHT)* The shape made here is similar to variation I of the Asymmetric Slit technique (*see* **page 31**), except that the angles of the creases are now asymmetric. Any form made using the Asymmetric Slit technique can be adapted to have asymmetrically placed creases as well.

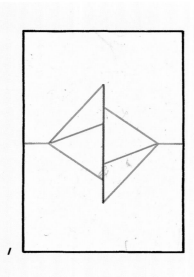

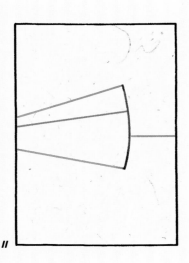

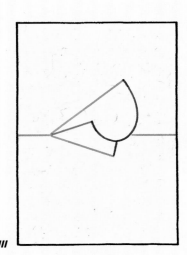

I

II

III

Generations

Each pop-up, it will be observed, is built on a single gutter crease, and when fully formed has created more creases. These new creases can in their turn be regarded as gutter creases and be used to generate more pop-ups, which in their turn will generate more creases, which in their turn can generate more pop-ups . . . and so on down through successive generations. By this technique, very complex forms can be created.

1 Fold a sheet of stiff paper in half. Using a
.. pencil, measure and mark the halfway point along the gutter crease, then draw a line from the gutter crease to the centre of the folded paper and cut it (*see* **fig 1**).

2 Fold the lower half of the sheet so that the
.. gutter crease and the edges meet exactly. Press firmly. Unfold this half of the paper, then open it out.

3 Create the pop-up by pulling up the lower
.. half of the card and forming a mountain crease. At the same time, close the paper shut again – all the creases must be created simultaneously.

4 Draw a second line from halfway down the
.. pop-up to halfway across to the right-hand edge. Cut along this line, making sure you cut through all four layers of paper (*see* **fig 2**).

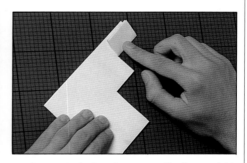

5 Crease as before (*see* **step 2**), then unfold
.. and open the sheet.

(continued . . .)

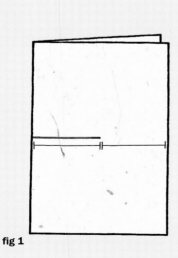

fig 1

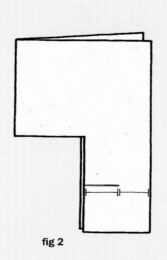

fig 2

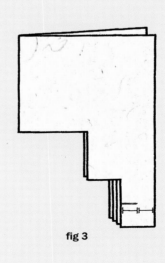

fig 3

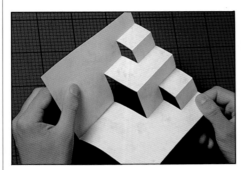

6 Form the mountain and valley creases as before (*see* **step 3**), to create another two pop-up shapes.

BELOW The pop-up could have more generations than the three shown here, each time doubling the number of pop-ups made.

7 As before, make a third cut from halfway down the new pop-up to halfway across to the right-hand edge. Crease as before (*see* **steps 2** *and* **3**), this time to create four smaller pop-ups (*see* **fig 3** *previous page*).

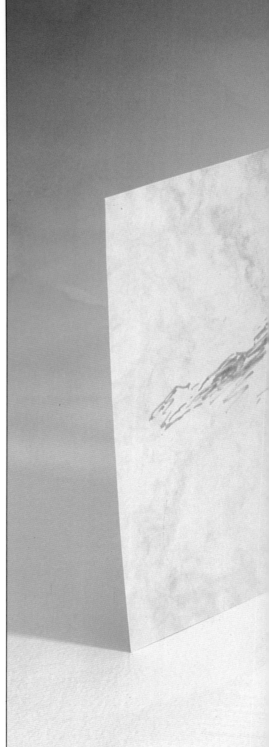

ALPINE SCENE

height 16 cm (6¼ in)

In this Alpine scene, the careful choice of an appropriately textured card (cardboard) contrasts well with the free pen drawing. The two generations give the design its structure, but in this example, the artwork is more important than the pop-up forms.

Generations Variation

This technique uses the same cuts and creases that were shown in the step-by-step sequence of the Angle of Crease, but instead of starting by creating one triangle, you double it up and create two.

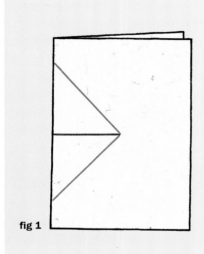

fig 1

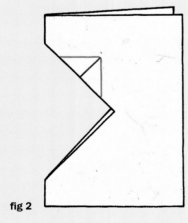

fig 2

RIGHT This simple but charming frog is really only three "mouths", the smaller, second generation mouths becoming eyes.

1 Fold a sheet of stiff paper in half. Draw a horizontal line from the gutter crease to the centre of the paper, then draw two triangle shapes (*see* **fig 1**). (Coloured lines have been used in this example, but you should draw in pencil). Cut along the horizontal line, then fold one triangle forwards along the crease lines. Press firmly, then repeat for the other triangle. Unfold both triangles, then fold them over backwards along the same crease lines.

2 Fold the triangles back to their original position and open out the paper. To form the pop-up, pull up both triangles, and at the same time close the paper again. All the creases must form together. You should end up with mountain creases down the centre of the triangles and all the rest as valleys.

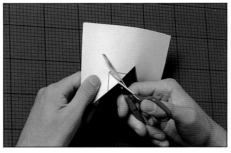

3 Draw a small perpendicular line from the upper pop-up, and then draw triangles to either side (*see* **fig 2**). Cut through all four layers of paper.

4 Repeat the folding and creasing sequence that you used for the first pop-ups (*see* **step 2**), creating miniature versions of the triangular pop-ups as before.

Cut Aways

Of all the basic one-piece pop-up techniques, Cut Aways is without doubt the most versatile and open-ended, but perhaps also the most difficult to master fully. Nevertheless, even a rudimentary understanding of this useful technique will add visual interest to the most basic pop-up. In essence, a cut away frees material at a crease so that it can rise away from the crease. It is best to draw the complete construction before cutting and creasing the pop-up.

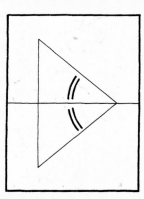

Do not crease the paper. Instead, use a pencil to draw the basic construction shown here. Note the equal angles on either side of the gutter crease.

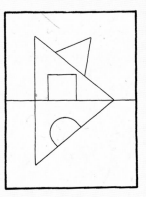

Draw three shapes, as shown, each beginning and ending on its own crease.

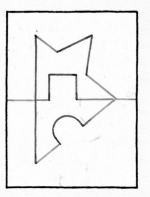

Erase from the construction that part of the crease which is within each shape. (For clarity, coloured lines have been used in this diagram to show which lines are for cutting and which are for folding.)

1 Having carefully drawn the construction, begin to slit, as shown. Then cut the semicircle, square and triangle.

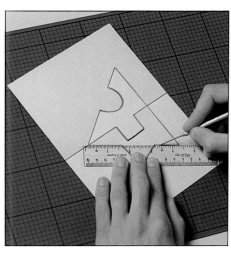

2 Indent or score the creases. Do not crease them by eye as this will not be accurate.

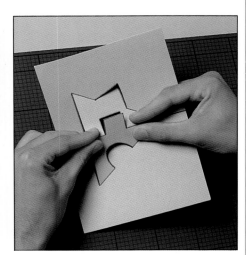

3 Begin to form the pop-up. Crease the red line as a mountain fold and the green lines as valley folds.

(continued . . .)

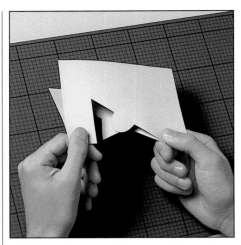

4 Flatten the creased pop-up and press it firmly to reinforce the creases.

"18"
height 15 cm (6 in)

BELOW *This design is not a pop-up in the conventional sense, but the four vertical creases permit the numerals to stand away from the mountain folds in a pop-up manner. The card (cardboard) for each numeral comes from the rear face of each pleat, neatly out of sight. The possibilities for layering designs in this way are endless.*

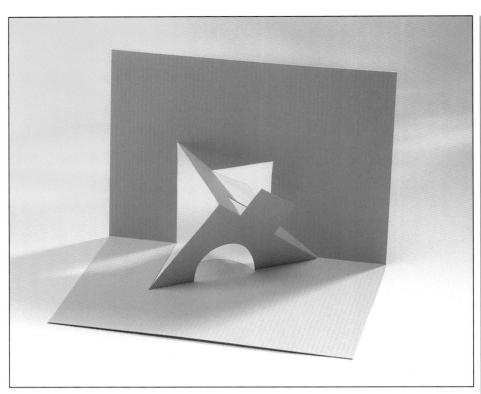

ABOVE Each shape stands unsupported, transforming an ordinary triangular pop-up into a complex and intriguing shape.

Angles of Creases

Double Slit

. . . .

Double Slit pop-ups are more than just two Single Slit pop-ups placed side by side; they offer entirely new technical possibilities. The categories that follow are similar to the Single Slit categories in the previous chapter, but the forms which are created are very different.

With this technique the shape of the two slits remains constant but the placement of the crease, or creases, may change.

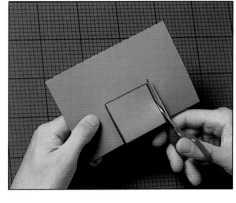

1.. Fold a sheet of stiff paper in half. Draw two horizontal lines from the gutter crease to the centre of the paper, then join them. Cut along the two horizontal lines. (For clarity, coloured lines have been used in this example, but you should draw in pencil.)

2.. Carefully make a crease between the two slits, folding the paper forwards.

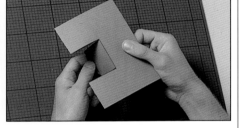

3.. Then fold the flap backwards along the same crease line.

4.. Unfold the flap back to its previous position, then open out the card.

5.. To form the pop-up, pull up the central section of the gutter crease to create a mountain. All the other creases remain as valleys. Close the pop-up shut and press it flat to strengthen all the creases.

Although this pop-up is made with two slits, it has the same number of creases as the Single Slit pop-ups described earlier.

Angles of Creases Variations

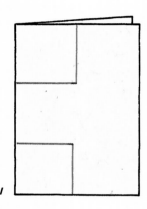

I

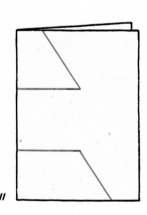

II

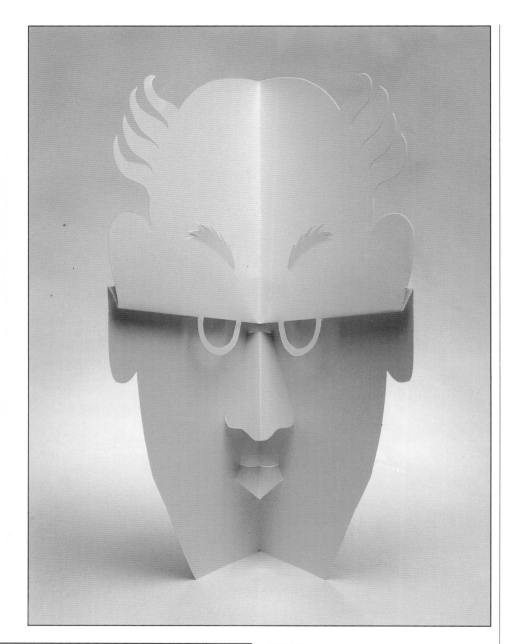

HEAD

height 26 cm (10¼ in)

ABOVE *This delightful design is made all the more effective by not being contained within a rectangular backing sheet. Note the conventional double slit pop-up forms at the nose and mouth. The spectacle frames are made using the Cut Away technique, extracting card from beneath the pleat across the brow.*

LEFT: *I (LEFT)* and *II (RIGHT)* In these two examples, the central section of the gutter crease remains untouched so that the pop-ups form above and below it.

Shapes of Slits

Just as the angles of the creases can change so can the shapes of the slits. These are just a very few of the many possibilities.

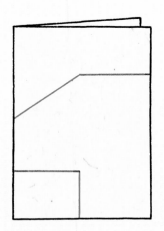

Draw the construction shown here. (For clarity, coloured lines have been used in this example, but you should use pencil.)

1 Having carefully drawn the construction, cut along the brown lines.

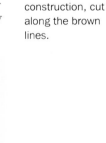

2 To form the pop-up, make two creases, folding the paper forwards and backwards along the red lines.

3 Open out the card and form the first simple step-shaped pop-up by pulling the step-shape upwards to create a mountain crease.

4 Then create the other, more complex pop-up by reinforcing the creases and closing the card simultaneously.

RIGHT The slits need not always run into the gutter crease.

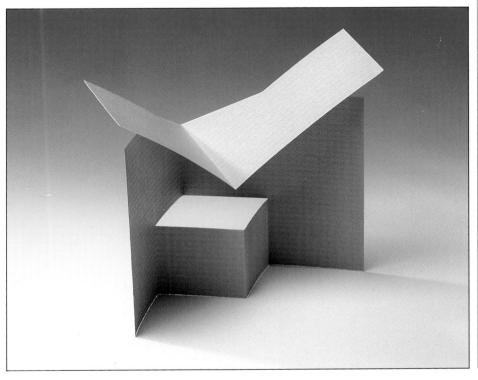

Shapes of Slits Variations

RIGHT: *I (LEFT)* In this example, the diagonal slits create a strong chevron shape. *II (RIGHT)* By carefully judging the angles of the pop-ups, shapes can be made to extend beyond the backing sheet.

BELOW: *III (LEFT)* When opened, the pop-up arms uncross themselves. *IV (RIGHT)* In this example, the pop-up pierces the plane of the backing sheet so that the construction looks as good from the back as from the front.

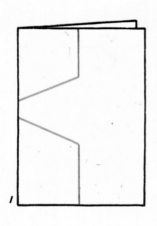

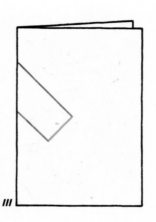
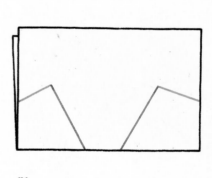

I

II

III

IV

CLOWN

height 30 cm (12 in)

The bright colours are achieved by a collage of coloured papers. Note how the clown is made to stand away from the backing sheet using just two symmetrical slits.

Asymmetric Slits

The preliminary construction is identical to that of the Single Slit version of the Asymmetric Slit technique (*see* **page 29**). Once the creases have been established, the two slits can be added.

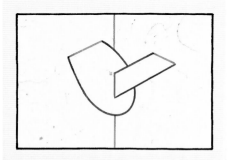

Using a pencil, draw the construction following the diagram. (For clarity, coloured lines have been used in this example to show which lines are for cutting and which are for creasing.)

BELOW By bringing the two slits across the gutter, a Cut Away effect can be created.

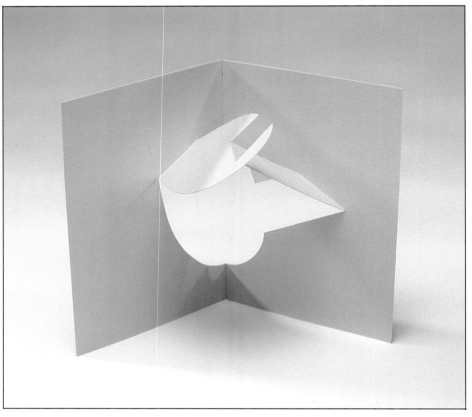

1 .. Having carefully drawn the construction, cut along the brown lines.

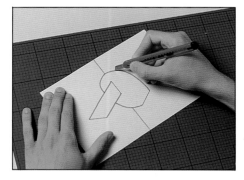

2 .. Indent or score the creases before actually creasing, otherwise it will be difficult to make them accurately. Begin to form the pop-up by creasing along the red line.

3 .. Lift the pop-up to form valleys along the green lines, then begin to close the backing sheet over it.

4 .. Flatten the creased pop-up and press it to reinforce the creases.

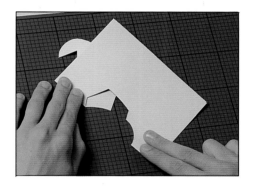

HORSE'S HEAD
height 21 cm (8¾ in)
*A careful construction of the form and its
placement within the structure of the
pop-up, make sophisticated use of a simple
technique. To give interest to the surface of
the card, watercolour pigment has been
brushed onto wet watercolour paper.*

Asymmetric Slits Variations

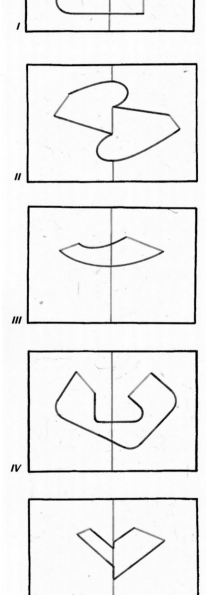

I (LEFT) Similar to variation II, the free-standing shapes are here placed on the "V" creases, except that these creases have rotated to become parallel. *II (CENTRE)* In this example, the slits create shapes that stand away from the gutter crease. Note, also, how the "V" creases do not reach the gutter crease. *III (RIGHT)* In this pop-up, two simple curves create an elegant swept form.

IV (LEFT) In this example, the pop-up shape is on the outside of the "V" creases, not on the inside as is more common. *V (RIGHT)* If the slits are cut partway along the gutter crease, one half of the pop-up can be made considerably smaller.

Asymmetric Mountain

Almost all the Single and Double Slit techniques so far explained have maintained a central mountain crease in line with the gutter crease behind it. However, this mountain may be moved away from the centre to create an asymmetric effect that is both elegant and surprising. Follow the step-by-step construction with care.

The Asymmetric Mountain technique can be used in the same way as conventional symmetrical techniques. The variations show some of these possibilities – remember to draw the complete construction *before* making any creases or cuts.

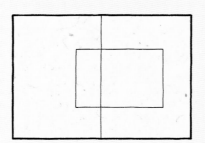

Using a pencil, draw a crease down the centre of a stiff piece of paper. Draw two horizontal lines that extend further to the right of the vertical line than to the left. Connect the horizontals with vertical lines, to form a rectangle.

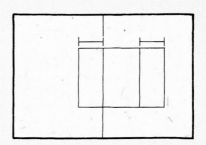

Measure the distance between the centre line and the vertical line to its left. Reproduce that distance, measuring it from the inside of the right-hand vertical. Draw another vertical line at this point.

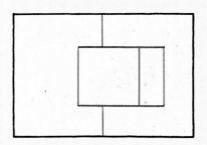

Erase the central section of the gutter crease. (For clarity, coloured lines have been used here to show which creases are for folding and which are for cutting.)

1 Having drawn the construction, cut along the brown lines using a craft knife.

2 Using an indenting tool and a ruler, indent all the creases, then begin to form the creases individually.

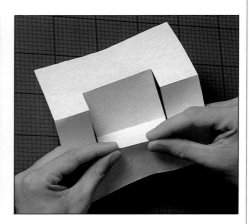

3 It is often easier to reinforce the creases from behind.

(continued . . .)

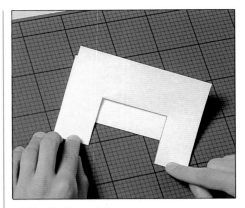

4 Finally, form all the creases
.. simultaneously, flattening the pop-up.
Press the pop-up firmly.

In this construction, note how one face of the
pop-up step is much longer than the other.

ROOM
height
15 cm (6 in)
*The shape of the
desk is a basic Step
form pop-up, but
the removal of
excess card
(cardboard) around
the legs and the
desk light (made
using the Cut Away
technique) creates
visual interest. The
wall is covered by a
textured wallpaper,
the floor by fabric,
and the desk by a
sticky-backed wood
grain covering paper
(contact paper).*

Asymmetric Mountain Variations

I (LEFT) The slits along the shorter step have been pushed up along the longer step, creating free-standing forms. *II (RIGHT)* In this example, the slits change direction at the mountain crease, creating a dramatic change of shape.

III (LEFT) The asymmetric mountain is here transformed into a valley where two Cut Away forms entwine. *IV (RIGHT)* As with other one-piece techniques, pop-up forms can be made to pierce the plane of the backing sheet.

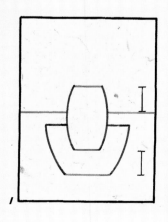
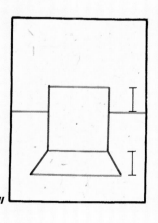
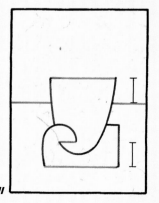
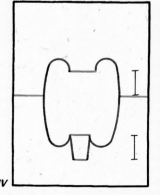

I   II   III   IV

Asymmetric Angles

The Double Slit version of this technique is only a little different from the simpler Single Slit version; the additional slit frees the second end of the pop-up, enabling it to stand away from the gutter crease. The construction must be drawn before making any cuts or creases. Draw the Single Slit Asymmetric Angle example (*see* **page 32**) up to the third diagram, then continue as below. You will need a protractor to make sure the angles are accurate.

Like the Asymmetric Mountain technique, Asymmetric Angles can also be used in the same way as conventional symmetrical techniques. Here are some examples; remember to draw the complete construction before making any creases or cuts.

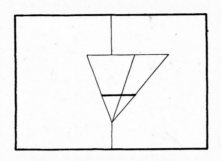

Using a pencil, draw a second horizontal line below the first, connecting the outer arms of the "V".

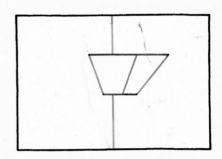

Erase all the lines that are below the horizontal line that you have just drawn. (For clarity, coloured lines have been used here to indicate which lines are for creasing and which for cutting.)

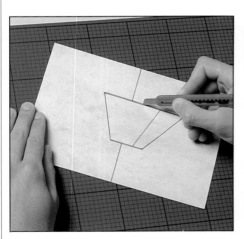

1 Having drawn the construction, cut along the brown lines using a craft knife.

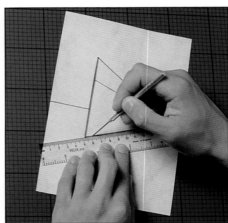

2 Using an indenting tool and a ruler, indent all the crease lines.

3 Form each of the creases individually. You may find it easier to reinforce some of them from the back of the sheet of paper.

ONE-PIECE TECHNIQUES

HOUSE
height
14 cm (5½ in)
Architectural forms make ideal subjects for the Asymmetric Angles technique, because the effects of perspective can be used to good advantage. The chimney is made using the Cut Away technique and the surface decoration is made using coloured pencils.

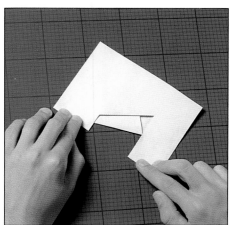

4 Finally, close the pop-up, forming all of the creases simultaneously. Flatten the pop-up and press the creases to reinforce them.

RIGHT The asymmetrical design gives a foreshortening effect.

Asymmetric Angles Variations

I (LEFT) The change of angle of the pop-up form at the mountain crease exaggerates the sense of distorted perspective that is common to most Asymmetric Angle pop-ups. *II (RIGHT)* Here, the curious angles that result from this technique are shown to good effect, transforming a pop-up that would be uninteresting if all the creases were parallel, into one with character.

IV (LEFT) This bizarre pop-up is not made inside the asymmetric creases but *outside*. Note how the mountain crease on the ring is in line with the mountain crease inside the conventional asymmetric configuration of creases. *IV (RIGHT)* For fun, the creases and slits are "textured" with the addition of small Cut Away shapes.

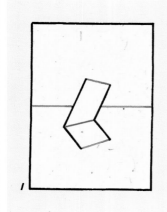

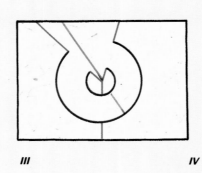

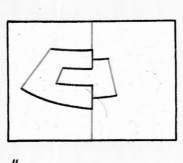

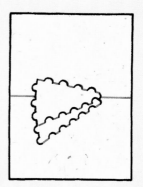

I   II   III   IV

Generations

Any pop-up form that straddles a gutter crease will in turn generate extra creases that can become new gutter creases to generate more pop-ups and so on. This technique, used with the Cut Away technique, is the most useful of all one-piece techniques, permitting the combination of any or all the preceding techniques, in whatever form. An understanding of its basic principles, and a little patience in construction, will eventually lead to a mastery of one-piece pop-ups.

The Generations technique has many applications. Each of the variations on page 57 highlights a major technical theme for the reader to explore.

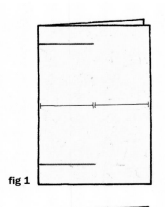

fig 1

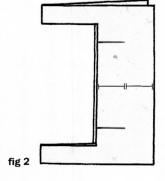

fig 2

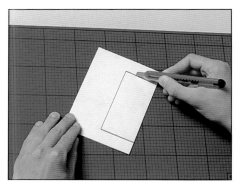

1 Fold a sheet of stiff paper in half. Draw two horizontal lines from the gutter crease (*see* **fig 1**) and join them. Cut along the horizontal lines. (For clarity, coloured lines have been used here, but you should draw in pencil.)

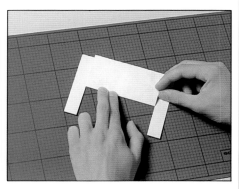

2 Make a crease between the ends of the slits, folding the paper forwards then backwards along the same line.

3 Open the sheet of paper. Create a conventional pop-up by pulling the step shape up while closing the card – all the creases must form simultaneously. The pop-up will have one mountain crease, and the rest are valleys.

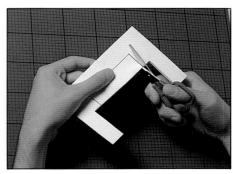

4 Close the pop-up again and repeat step 1 (*see* **fig 2**). You should cut through all four layers of paper, ending halfway across the remainder of the sheet.

5 Repeat step 2 and crease between the ends of the slits. Open the paper out once again.

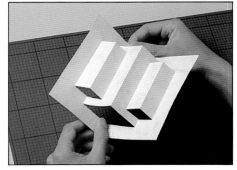

6 Create two new smaller pop-ups, using the same method as in step 3.

(continued . . .)

DOUBLE SLIT

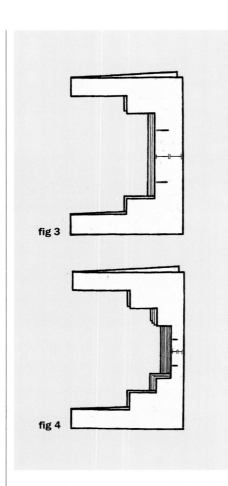

fig 3

fig 4

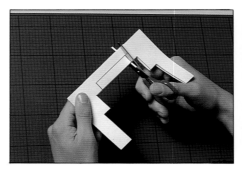

7 Repeat the procedure, this time to make four new pop-ups (*see* **fig 3**).

8 And repeat again, this time to make eight new pop-ups (*see* **fig 4**).

RIGHT This is the spectacular result. Given a large enough sheet of paper, the four generations made here could be extended to five, six or even more, with each new generation doubling the number of steps.

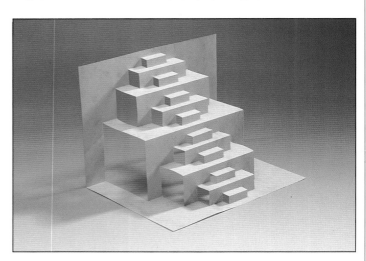

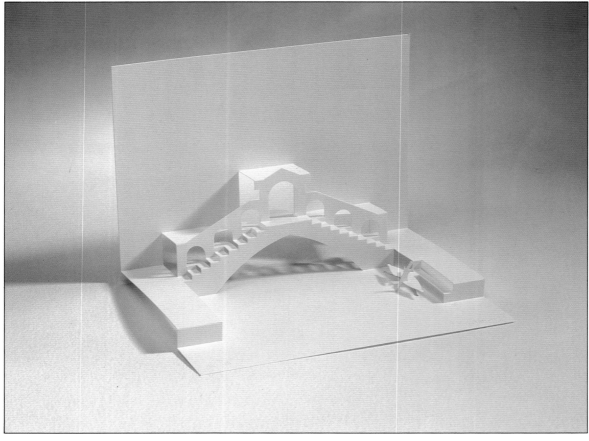

BRIDGE OF SIGHS
height
11cm (4¾ in)
The sophisticated use of the Generations technique, frequently coupled here with the Cut Away technique, creates a convincing sculptural effect. Note how the gondolier in the right foreground gives a sense of scale to the bridge.

Generations Variations

I (LEFT) Each generation falls away from the previous one to create an interesting spiral effect, in which the gutter crease gradually reverses on itself. *II (RIGHT)* In this example, the two generations use Asymmetric Mountain techniques. Note that the smallest pop-up is built across the mountain crease of the largest pop-up to create not a "pop-up", but its visual opposite, which might be termed as a "push in".

III (LEFT) The second-generation pop-ups to the left and to the right, line up against the central pushed-in area to create not three separate pop-ups, but one large one which becomes bigger than the initial first generation. *IV (CENTRE)* All these pop-ups are constructed using the Asymmetric Angles technique. Note that the second-generation pop-up on the right joins onto the large first-generation pop-up. *V (RIGHT)* In this example, each generation cuts into the previous one. Note how the location of each mountain crease is calculated.

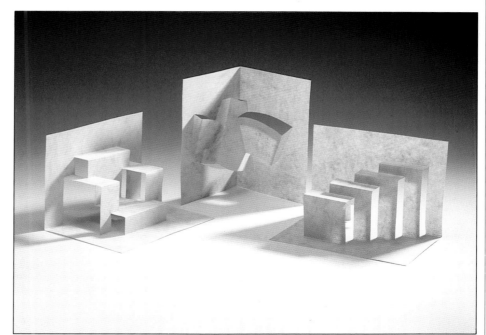

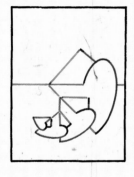

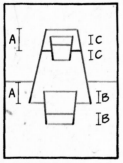

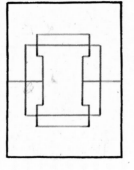

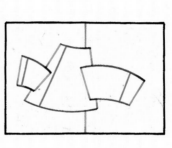

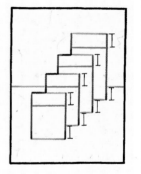

I II III IV V

Cut Aways

It is with this final basic technique that the art of designing one-piece pop-ups becomes almost open-ended, the only limitations being one's imagination. The variations on page 59 highlight some of the more basic Cut Away themes, but there are many others.

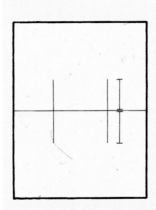

Using a pencil, draw a line across the centre of the paper. Then, draw two more vertical lines equidistant from the gutter crease.

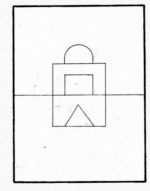

Join these lines to create a rectangle. Then draw three shapes, one on each vertical line.

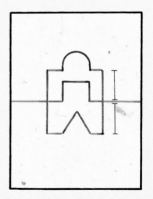

Erase all the excess lines. (For clarity, coloured lines have been used in this example to show which lines are for cutting and which are for folding.)

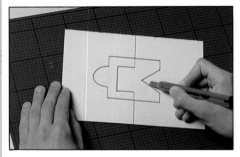

1 Having carefully drawn the construction, cut along the brown lines. Note that there are two long cuts as well as the semicircle, square and triangle.

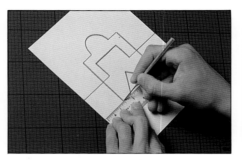

2 Using an indenting tool and a ruler, indent all the creases.

3 Form all the creases individually. You may find it easier to create some of the creases from the back.

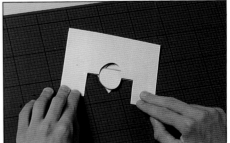

4 Finally, forming all the creases simultaneously, flatten the pop-up. Press the creases to reinforce them.

LEFT The three Cut Aways are seen here rising from three creases in a basic step form pop-up. Note how each Cut Away creates a negative (empty) shape where it has been cut away, as well as the positive shape of the Cut Away form.

Cut Aways Variations

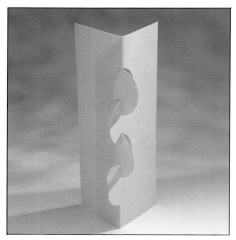

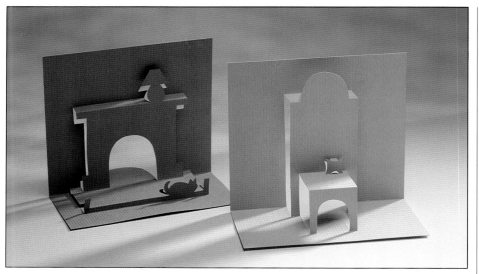

I If Cut Aways are placed along a single crease, they overlap to form a curious dovetail-joint effect. Note which creases are mountains and which are valleys.

II (LEFT) Two basic asymmetrical block forms (the hearth and fireplace) have had Cut Aways introduced to animate an otherwise simple geometric composition. The transformation of a geometric pop-up into one that is representational is often simpler than you

might at first imagine. *III (RIGHT)* Here, two generations of conventional blocks have been transformed into a chair with a cushion. Note the Cut Aways at the top of the chair back, at the top and the bottom of the cushion, and between the front legs.

DOVES
height 30 cm (12 in)

BELOW *This beautiful semi-abstract repeat design makes full use of the Cut Away technique to create a sense of negative/*

positive silhouettes. By using more than one crease, the pattern can be made to extend sideways, to establish the repeat.

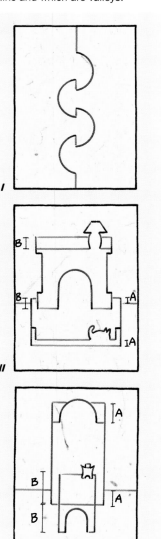

Other Techniques

The techniques that follow do not readily fit into the mainstream one-piece techniques described, yet they form an important part of the vocabulary. As you will have observed, no technique is entirely distinct from all others so you will find in this section that many overlap with earlier techniques. Indeed, it is curious how one technique mutates into another, particularly when Generations and Cut Aways are used.

Multi Slit

After Single and Double Slit techniques, the obvious extension is to use Multi Slits. The technique is ideal for creating beautiful rhythmic abstracts, but much of their success depends on accurate measurements, so take time to draw them up and construct them with care!

1 Fold a stiff piece of paper in half. Using a
.. pencil, carefully draw, then cut, a series of parallel lines, creating a step effect. Note that the two longest lines are the same length.

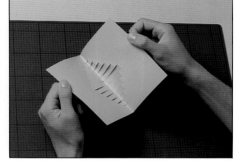

2 Begin the creasing by folding back each
.. step one at a time.

3 Make sure that all the strips lie neatly side
.. by side.

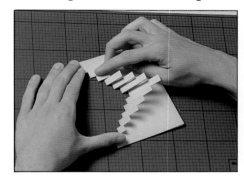

4 Fold all the steps backwards in the same
.. way, then open the paper.

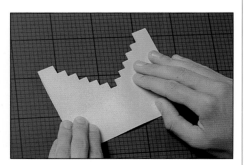

5 Create a series of conventional pop-ups,
.. one below the other, by carefully lifting and creasing the steps one at a time.

6 Close the pop-up and press it firmly to
.. reinforce all the creases.

RIGHT The narrower the strips, the better the pop-up looks, though if they are too narrow, they become weak and the pop-up looks deflated instead of pert.

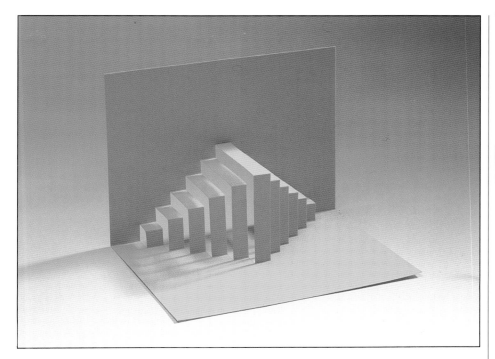

TIERED ABSTRACT

height 11 cm (4¾ in)

BELOW *The many slits of this remarkable pop-up create the illusion of a number of tiered semicircles. Although the effect is complex, the structure is based on two simple constraints: the length of each slit and the width of the paper between them.*

Multi Slit Variations

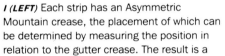

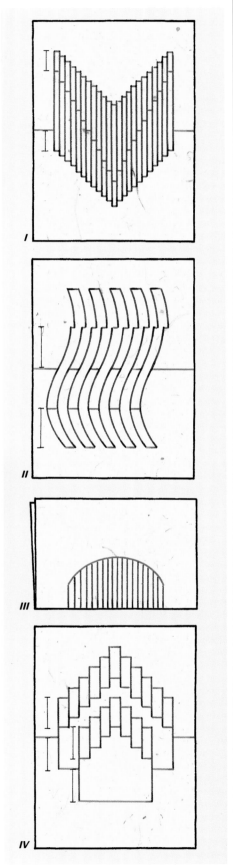

I (LEFT) Each strip has an Asymmetric Mountain crease, the placement of which can be determined by measuring the position in relation to the gutter crease. The result is a pleasing twisted form. *II (RIGHT)* Not every part of the sheet needs to be lifted to become part of a sequence of strips. Here, only every alternate one is lifted.

III (LEFT) Here, the strips are not folded in parallel but are allowed to splay out. *IV (RIGHT)* A platform of any shape can be supported by a series of strips. Note how the second generation is formed. The pop-up looks good whether it is on its base or side.

Steps

This is probably the single most fascinating and addictive one-piece technique! Once the basic measurement principles have been grasped, endless variations suggest themselves. To speed up construction, stick squared paper to the back of the card and draw the measurements onto it.

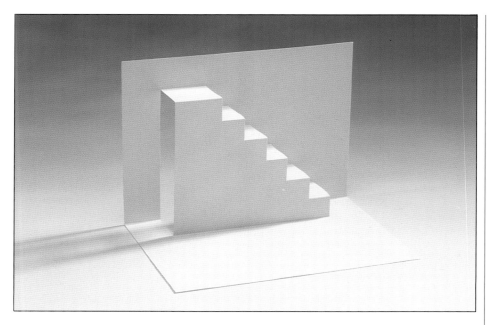

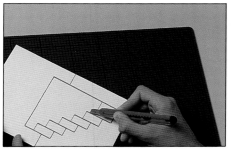

1 Having carefully drawn the construction, cut along the parallel lines.

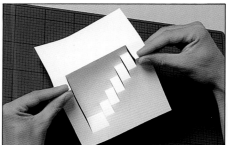

2 Use an indenting tool to go over all the creases, being careful to differentiate valleys from mountains. Then carefully form all the creases simultaneously to collapse the steps into their final shape.

ABOVE This is the basic Steps form. Note which of the distances are equal and how the mountain and valley creases touch the slits.

3 This is how the pop-up should look when the creasing is completed.

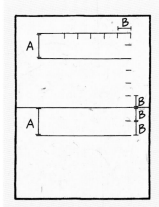 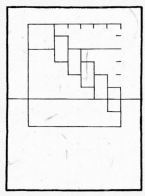 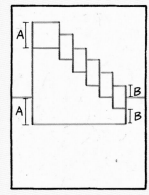

On a sheet of thin card (cardboard) and using a pencil, draw the gutter crease across the centre. Measure a square grid seven units wide and eight high. Note that the length of **A** is twice **B**.

Using the grid as a guide, draw the steps, as shown. Your drawing must be extremely accurate.

Erase all of the lines that are not needed for the construction. (For clarity, coloured lines have been used in this example to show which lines are for cutting and which for creasing.)

4 Finally, flatten the pop-up and press all the creases firmly.

Steps Variations

RIGHT: *I (LEFT)* In this example, a second generation is built onto the first. Note how both sets of steps appear less weighty than before because the front walls have been cut away at 45 degrees. *II (RIGHT)* A simple stage set can be constructed using the Steps technique. Note the cut aways beneath and on the stage, and at the door. More complex scenery could be added at the back.

LEFT: *III (LEFT)* As with most techniques, if the first generation is large enough, a second generation can be built in the front. Further generations can also be made. *IV (RIGHT)* Steps may also be linked, as shown here. In more complex pop-ups, intricately connected paths can be traced up and down the steps.

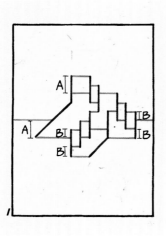

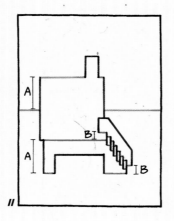

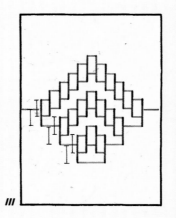

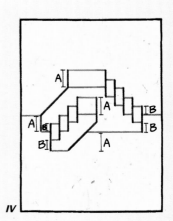

UNTITLED ABSTRACT

height 22 cm (8½ in)

The stunning effect of this design is achieved by the subtle use of two gutter creases, one a mountain, the other a valley. Each of these creates half the pop-up. The two halves meet down the centre to create a continuous ripple of steps.

Wings

This delightful technique is one of the simplest and perhaps the most artistic of one-piece techniques. This is because the outline of the two halves can be cut to almost any shape and the halves may join in many ways, thus permitting a remarkable amount of technical freedom. It is the only one-piece technique where glue is occasionally used.

1 Having carefully drawn the construction, make the two three-sided cuts.

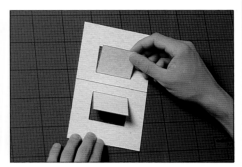

2 Indent or score the valley creases, then pull the two shapes upwards.

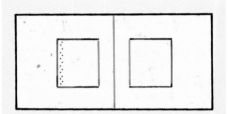

Divide a sheet of stiff paper down the middle, then using a pencil, draw two parallel lines equidistant and about 1-1.5 cm (½-¾ in) away from the centre. Draw two shapes, each beginning and ending on one of the outer lines. Erase the excess lines. (For clarity, coloured lines have been used in this example, to indicate which lines are for cutting and which are for folding.)

3 Glue the top edges together so that the construction will fold flat when it is closed.

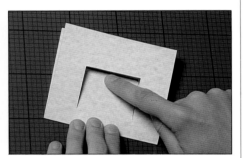

4 Fold the pop-up in half so that the glued edge sticks firmly to the opposite surface.

RIGHT If the holes are a visual distraction, the card can be backed onto a sheet of paper the same colour.

Wings Variations

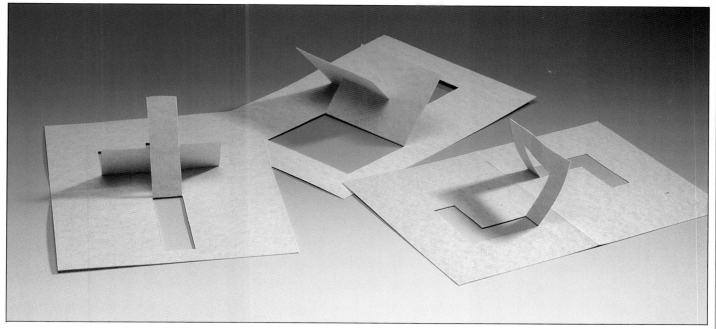

ABOVE: *I (LEFT)* The shapes need not be identical, nor indeed similar. They can be as diverse as the subject dictates. *II (CENTRE)* Here, the two halves are not directly opposite each other, but stepped. Note the slits that join them; no glue is used. *III (RIGHT)* In this instance the arms are glued together to form an arch which crosses the gutter crease at an angle.

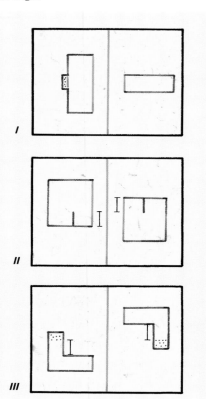

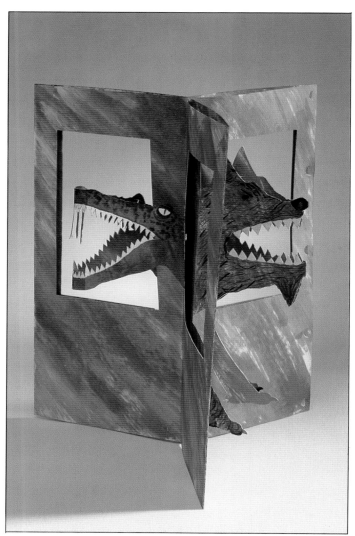

MONSTERS
height
26 cm (10¼ in)
The Wings technique is used three times to create the three monster heads (one is out of sight, at the back). The pop-up is made from a continuous, six-panel zig-zag of card (cardboard), folded to make the three-finned design seen here. To help make the heads clearly visible, excess card has been removed from around each head to create a series of rectangular windows. The card was painted with gouache.

Multi-piece Techniques

In contrast to one-piece designs, multi-piece pop-ups are often seen as less "pure", or somehow easier to create and construct. After all, it must surely be easier to create a pop-up by adding more and more pieces, than to achieve the same effect from a single sheet. In one way this is true, but the problems then become those of choice of techniques, and how to control these on the backing sheet. Like all creative problems, once the parameters are widened, the activity becomes technically and intellectually more difficult.

Nevertheless, multi-piece techniques are surprisingly easy to master, and will produce a variety of interesting forms with little effort. The techniques are more diverse than the one-piece techniques – each has its own method of construction, and one should not be confused with another. The forms that each technique can make are also more diverse, which makes it difficult for beginners properly to grasp the full potential of multi-piece pop-ups. However, to aid comprehension, it is important to understand the essential differences between the techniques and why they will collapse flat or erect. And it is more important to grasp the *principle* behind the exercises than the specifics: if the principle is understood, it can be applied to many more forms than the few shown in this book.

Multi-piece pop-ups must be made with precision. If they are carelessly made, they will neither collapse, nor fully erect.

To keep the smooth transition from two dimensions to three, it is important to construct a rigid backing sheet. A sheet that buckles or bends under strain as the pop-up above it erects, is too weak to be useful and must be stiffened. It is important to make a backing sheet of the right strength, and also to construct the pop-up itself from paper and/or card (cardboard) of the appropriate weight. As a general rule, thick paper or thin card is a good weight for a pop-up. See the Basics chapter (**page 17**), for instructions on how to construct a sturdy backing sheet.

In this chapter, templates are given for the shapes. Although these can be drawn to any size, it is important that the separate elements of the design remain in proportion with each other.

OPPOSITE
FISHES
height 20 cm (8 in)
This pop-up is made out of watercolour paper and decorated with gouache. The delicacy with which the card (cardboard) has been cut, and the minute detail of the painting, create a pop-up of exquisite intricacy. Technically though, it could hardly be simpler: a basic Trellis technique makes the "X" shape with a solid back, and a few small fish have been added to create extra layers of visual interest.

Horizontal "V" I

This technique is the simplest and most useful of all multi-piece techniques. Almost any reasonably sturdy, self-supporting shape can be made to stand with the simple addition of glue tabs across the bottom and a vertical crease. There are two basic ways to fix the pop-up shape to the backing sheet: the first is where the glue tabs across the bottom are glued directly onto the backing sheet; the second is where the tabs are pushed through slots to lie neatly out of sight beneath the backing sheet.

The first method is the simpler of the two, but it does, however, leave the glue tabs visible on the surface of the backing sheet, which can be unsightly if the papers do not match.

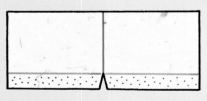

fig 1

1 Crease a hem across the foot of a rectangle of stiff paper. This hem will be the glue tab and it must always be accurately made for the technique to work (*see* **fig 1**).

2 Unfold the hem so that you have a valley crease.

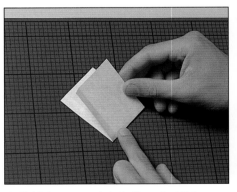

3 Fold the rectangle in half, so that if the hem crease is a valley, the new crease will be a mountain.

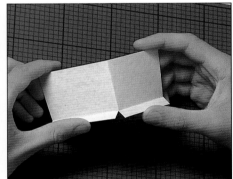

4 Unfold it. Make a slit up the mid crease to the hem crease to separate the hem into two "feet". This is the basic unit, ready to be glued to its backing sheet.

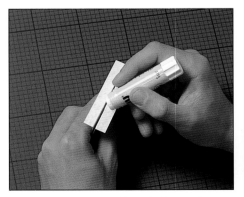

5 Close the pop-up and apply glue to the underside of both feet.

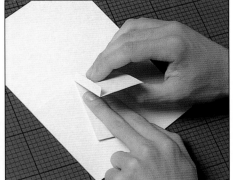

6 Very carefully glue one foot to the backing crease so that the point of the base of the pop-up where the feet meet *exactly touches* the gutter crease on the backing sheet. Note that the second foot is on top of the construction, glue side up.

7 Fold the backing sheet in half so that the second glued foot sticks to the empty side of the sheet.

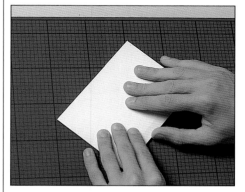

8 Press down on the pop-up to strengthen the adhesion of both feet to the backing sheet, then open it up.

Note how by following the above sequence of construction, the pop-up automatically folds flat, and that the two feet will always be at equal angles either side of the gutter crease.

VICTORIAN MAN
height
16 cm (6¼ in)
When closed, the Horizontal "V" crease across the neck swivels the head inside the pop-up, to lie over the tie. Note how much of the surface is drawn, not with lines, but with light and shade falling over the layered card. The effect, though subtle, is surprisingly clear.

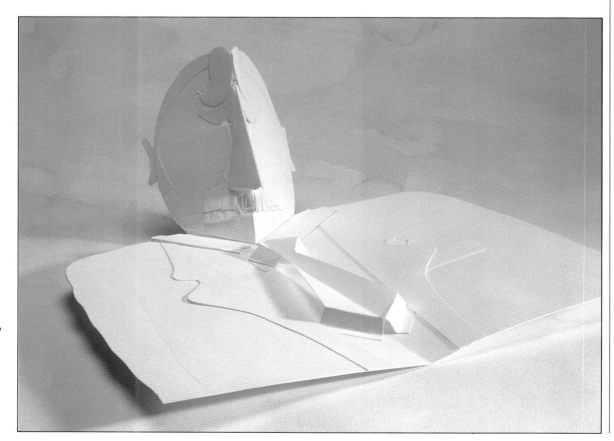

Horizontal "V" II

The first method is quick and simple, but for a neater finish the glue tabs ought to be hidden. The first method is ideal for roughs, and this second method for finished cards.

There are a good many different possibilities using this versatile technique, most of them related to the angles between the mid crease and the glue tabs. The variations that follow the step-by-step sequence cover some of the major themes.

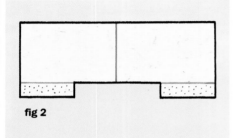

fig 2

1 Begin with the basic pop-up form, made in
.. steps 1 to 3 of the previous method (*see* **fig 1, page 70**).

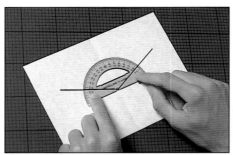

3 On the backing sheet, use a protractor to
.. measure equal angles each side of the gutter so that they form a "V". Draw in the angles. (For clarity, coloured lines have been used in this example, but you should draw them in pencil.)

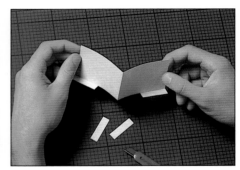

2 Cut away the central area of the glue tabs.
.. The precise amount cut off is unimportant, but neither tab should encroach too closely on the mid crease (*see* **fig 2**).

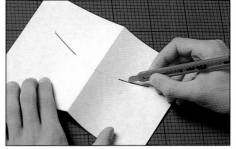

4 Turn the backing sheet over and cut slots
.. to correspond with the positions and lengths of the glue tabs on the pop-up unit.

5 Turn the backing sheet over again and
.. push the glue tabs through the slots.

6 Fasten each tab flat with a length of sticky
.. tape or glue. Open out the sheet.

LEFT The glue tabs, now beneath the backing sheet, are not visible. The central sections of the tabs were cut away so that the slots would not meet at the gutter crease, and thereby creating an unnecessarily weak backing sheet.

Horizontal "V" Variations

I (REAR LEFT) The conventional "V" form can be changed so that one half overhangs the other. Note the discreet triangle, small but essential. *II (REAR RIGHT)* The mid crease need not be vertical, but can fall at an angle to create an interesting, twisted, asymmetric form. *III (FRONT LEFT)* The tab crease is not horizontal, but v-shaped. When stuck to a backing sheet, it creates a pop-up that is sloping, not vertical as before. *IV (FRONT RIGHT)* Here, part of the pop-up unit has been cut away to create an arched form. Be particularly careful when gluing it to the backing sheet, as the point where the mid crease meets the tab crease has been cut away and therefore must be imagined.

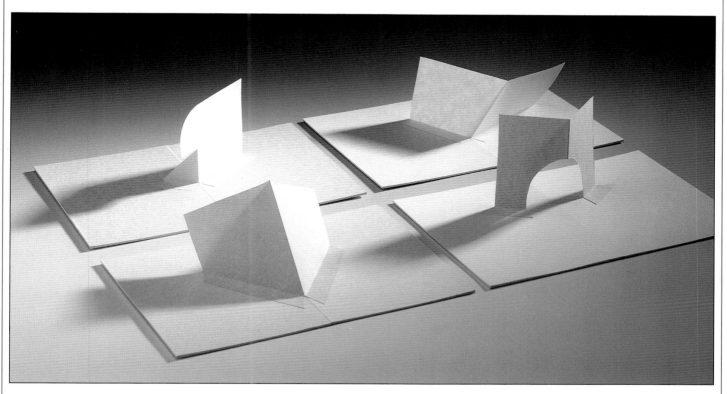

RIGHT: *V* This is perhaps the most dramatic of all pop-up effects: that of creating a large shape which springs up over the top edge of the backing sheet when it is opened.

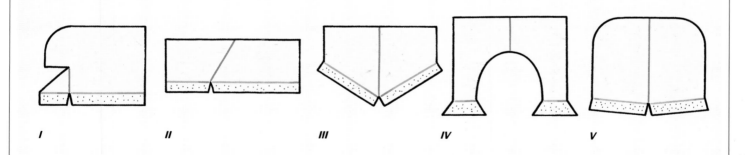

I   II   III   IV   V

Floating Layers

Many pop-up techniques create forms that can look firmly grounded, even heavy and blocklike. By contrast, this Floating Layers technique creates forms that appear to float unsupported in mid-air. They take careful preparation to make, but the effect is always worthwhile.

The Floating Layers effect has two elements; the supports and the layer itself. They are made separately. First make the backing sheet (*see* **page** 17), then start constructing this design by making the supports, and follow with the layer afterwards.

As the variations that follow the step-by-step sequence show, the Floating Layers principle can be applied in many ways, though there must always be at least three supports, one along the gutter crease and one to each side.

Cut a strip of medium-weight paper to an 18 x 6 cm (7 x 2½ in) rectangle and crease two hems 1 cm (½ in) from the top and bottom edges.

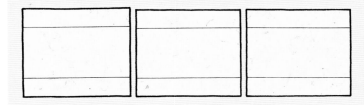

Cut the strip into three 6 cm (2½ in) lengths.

1 Fold each strip, as shown here. If the horizontal creases are mountains, fold a valley down the centre. Make a slit up the mid crease of each strip, to separate the hem and create two "feet".

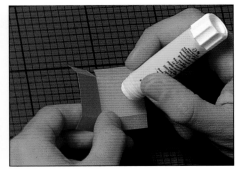

2 For each support, apply glue to one half of the inner face.

3 Close the support, pressing the two faces together. This shows one support complete.

4 Carefully glue the base of one support *exactly* over the gutter crease on the backing sheet.

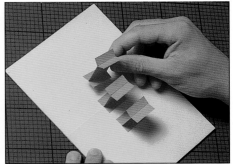

5 Glue down the other two, in line with the first support.

MULTI-PIECE TECHNIQUES

6 Cut the floating layer out of a sheet of stiff
.. paper. It should be large enough to cover
the supports. Crease it down the middle.
Apply glue to the central support *only* and
carefully join the central crease of the layer to
the central crease of the support.

7 Apply glue to the other supports, then
.. flatten all three to the left, being careful
not to let the glue touch the underside of the
floating layer.

8 Lower the layer onto the glued supports
.. so that the whole structure is flat. Then
carefully pull it upright.

BELOW Although the method may seem
lengthy, it is not difficult. The unsightly feet at
the base of the supports can be made
invisible if the backing sheet is slit and the feet
pushed through.

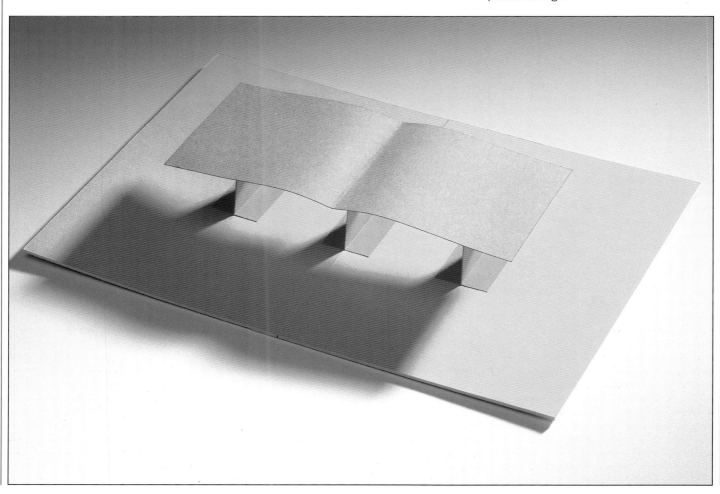

Floating Layers Variations

RIGHT: *I (LEFT)* Not only can the floating layer be any reasonable shape, but the crease can pass across it at any angle. Once this is understood, the technique has great versatility, even when used very simply, as here. *II (RIGHT)* Any pop-up technique can be constructed to rise from the floating layer as though the layer were the backing sheet. Indeed, layer can be built on layer to resemble a tiered cake.

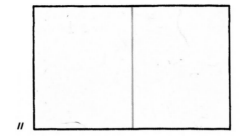

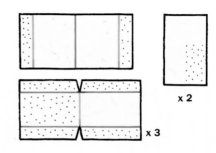

x 2

x 3

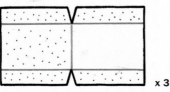

x 3

I

BUTTERFLY

height 5 cm (2 in)

This charming design sees the butterfly naturally open its wings when the pop-up is opened. The black shading on the hand and butterfly is achieved by the designer photocopying his own hand and a black and white illustration of a butterfly. The colour was added with marker pens.

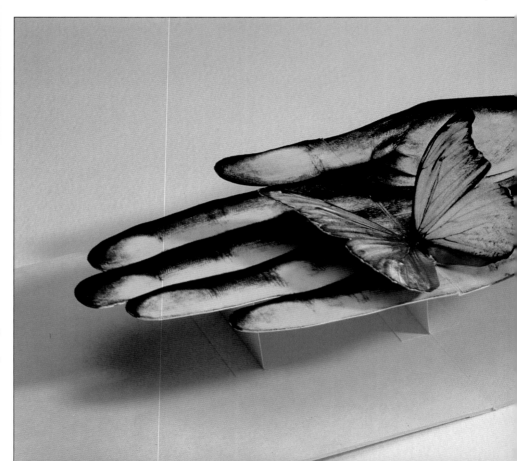

ABOVE: *III* For simplicity of construction, the outer supports and the floating layer on top can be made from one piece of paper. Once constructed, the form can be used to support a great many auxiliary shapes.

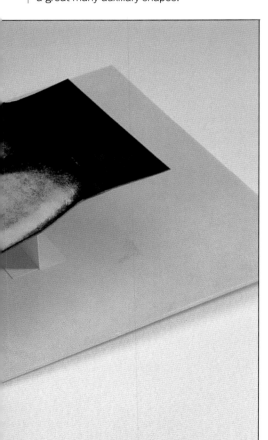

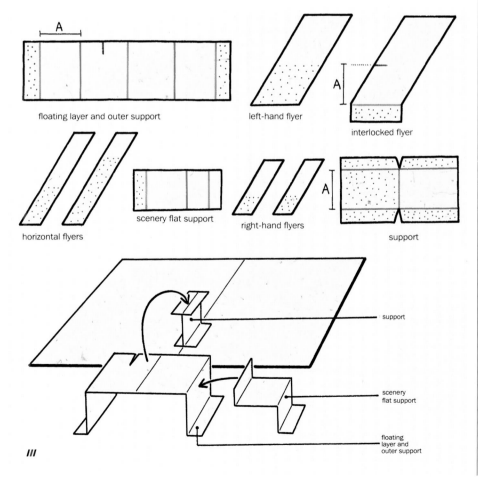

floating layer and outer support

left-hand flyer

interlocked flyer

horizontal flyers

scenery flat support

right-hand flyers

support

support

scenery flat support

floating layer and outer support

III

Scenery Flats

Though included here in the 180-degree techniques section, Scenery Flats are 90-degree techniques, but made with several pieces. Essentially, any two planes that meet can be used to support a flat. For the technique to work well, the flat and its supporting tab must be accurately positioned.

Scenery flats are an ideal and simple way to create multi-layered effects, but remember that the more layers that you place in front of one another, the less "power" there will be available to erect them all when the gutter crease is opened.

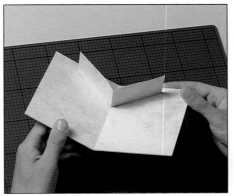

1 Make a conventional Horizontal "V" pop-up **..** (*see* **page 70**). This creates the 90-degree angle between the backing sheet and the wall, which is necessary for the scenery flat to collapse flat.

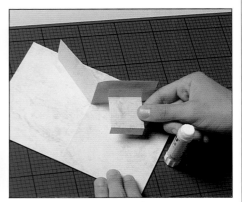

2 Make a supporting tab following the **..** instructions on the template drawing (*see* **fig 1**). Glue it to the wall, parallel to the backing sheet.

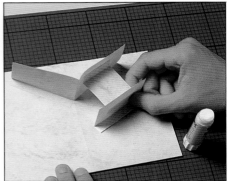

3 Measure the horizontal length of the tab **H**, **..** and the vertical distance between the backing sheet and the tab **V** (*see* **fig 2**). Glue the scenery flat to the front of the tab in such a position that the **H** and **V** distances are reproduced along the backing sheet and beneath the front of the tab. Therefore, the tab is parallel to the backing sheet and the flat is parallel to the walls.

LEFT The flat is located on the valley side of the "V" and will fall forwards when the backing sheet is closed.

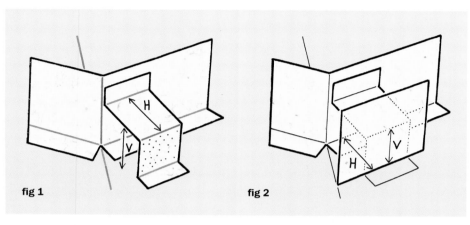

fig 1

fig 2

NEIGHBOURS
height 14 cm (5½ in)

BELOW *The use of acetate to connect each neighbour to the wall makes the tabs all but invisible, and hence not as intrusive on the design as card (cardboard) would have been. Another alternative is to use cotton thread. The surface design was painted using gouache.*

Scenery Flats Variations

I (REAR LEFT) A supporting tab can be slit at points along its length to support flats, which are also slit at the appropriate corresponding points and interlocked into the tab. This intricate layering effect has many uses. *II (REAR RIGHT)* The support need not be at 90 degrees to the backing sheet; then the flats will lie at an angle to the backing sheet. *III (FRONT RIGHT)* Using the measurement principles described in the Asymmetric Angles technique, flats can be added that are not parallel to a backing wall but at an angle, thereby creating a more interesting visual effect. In this case, the support should be glued to the backing sheet in the position shown in diagram III. *IV (FRONT LEFT)* Flats can be added to each side of a supporting wall located on the gutter crease. The flats to each side must be approximately equal, or the central wall will lean to one side when the gutter is unfolded.

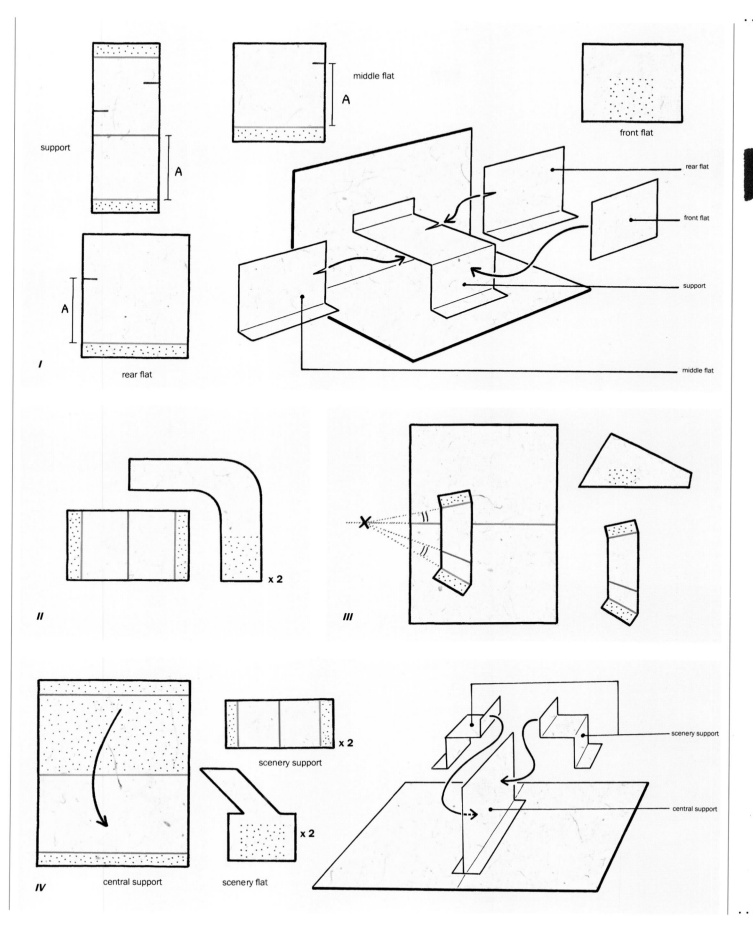

support

middle flat

A

A

front flat

rear flat

front flat

support

middle flat

I

rear flat

x 2

II

X

III

central support

scenery support

x 2

x 2

scenery flat

scenery support

central support

IV

Straps

The Straps technique, though simple, is rarely used in professional pop-up books and greetings cards because it can occupy too much valuable space. Nevertheless, its advantage is that it can create pop-ups that are to one side of the gutter crease, which increases the surprise when the card is opened.

1 Cut out a rectangle of stiff paper. Add a
.. central mountain crease and two
equidistant valleys.

2 Glue the strap onto a sturdy backing sheet
.. so that the mountain crease lies directly
over the gutter crease. This is the strap
complete.

3 To complete the
.. off-centre effect,
glue Horizontal "V"
walls (*see* **page 70**)
across the valley
creases. Note that
the strap is flat
across the gutter
crease.

BELOW The extra valley creases generated by
a strap can be used to power pop-ups *of any
technique*; Horizontal "V", Floating Layers and
so forth.

Straps Variations

I (LEFT) With the valley creases now almost (but not exactly) perpendicular to the gutter crease, the axis of the pop-up becomes even more twisted away from being parallel to the gutter crease. *II (RIGHT)* Glue the strap to the backing sheet. Regard the right-hand valley crease on the strap as a gutter crease, and glue the pop-up across it using the method described in the Horizontal "V" technique (*see* **page 72**). Because the valley strap creases are not parallel to the gutter crease, the pop-up is twisted to an unexpected position. Note how the pop up overhangs the back of the strap.

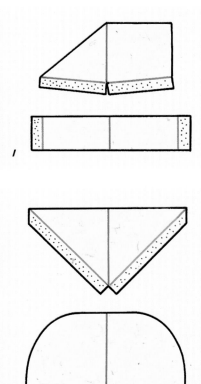

LOCH NESS MONSTER
height 13 cm (5 in)
LEFT *The Straps technique is used here to create a pop-up head and hump, but with a flat gutter crease between them. Pens and pencils were used to decorate the monster and a swirling marble-effect paper makes a convincingly cold-looking loch.*

Diagonal Box

Pop-up boxes can be made in many different ways and can have many different shapes. They are particularly satisfying to make, because unlike other pop-up techniques, they can create an illusion of volume. From the simple starting point shown in this step-by-step sequence and the variations, many fascinating forms can be developed.

TULIP
height 10 cm (4 in)
Four flat sheets of card (cardboard) slot together to make what is essentially a square box, fixed to the gutter crease using the Diagonal Box technique. *The use of slots, rather than creases, means that the tulip opens very easily when the card is opened.*

Draw the diagram on a sheet of stiff paper, carefully measuring the four equal panels and noting the glue tabs. (For clarity, coloured lines have been used in this example, but you should use pencil.)

1 Having drawn the diagram, cut out the box
.. shape. Next, fold the panels, creasing the red lines as mountain folds and the green lines as valley folds.

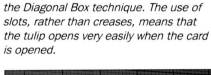

2 Fold the panels to create a square tube.
.. Glue the end tab to secure the shape.

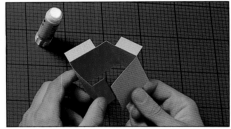

3 Glue the underside of the remaining tabs.
.. Open the tube to a perfect square, so that the gutter crease on the backing sheet connects *exactly* with opposite corners of the square, then press the glued tabs to the backing sheet. (If the tabs are unsightly, slit the backing sheet and push them through out of sight.)

LEFT The taller the tube becomes, the less upright it will stand.

Diagonal Box Variations

I (LEFT) Here, the walls of the box support a tall "X" form. Note that each half of the "X" has two glue tabs and the distance between them is the length of the side of the box. When gluing the tall units into the box be careful to glue them exactly to the middles of the four sides. *II (CENTRE)* The walls of the box can be used to support scenery flats. Note the interlocking triangle using the Trellis technique. *III (RIGHT)* By elongating the box, it can become rectangular. As in variation I, it can be further subdivided.

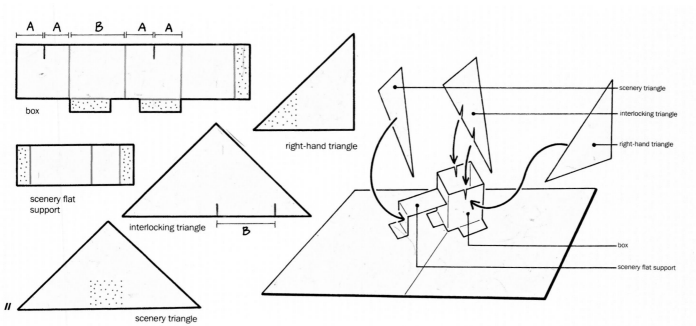

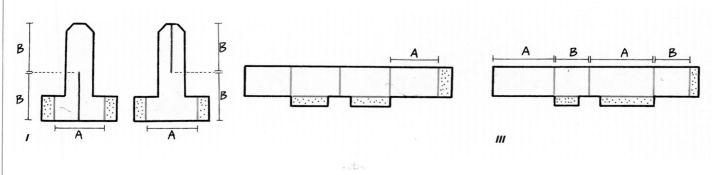

I

III

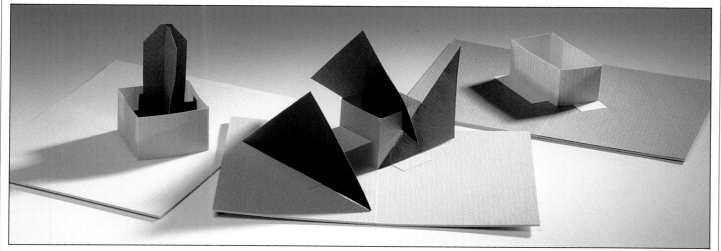

box

scenery flat support

interlocking triangle

II scenery triangle

right-hand triangle

scenery triangle

interlocking triangle

right-hand triangle

box

scenery flat support

Square-on Box

The construction is very similar to that of the Diagonal Box, but there are two extra vertical creases and the two tabs are placed differently. The orientation of the Square-on Box creates a different geometry and a new set of pop-up possibilities.

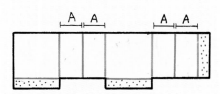

Using a pencil, draw the diagram on a sheet of stiff paper. (For clarity, coloured lines have been used in this example to show which lines are valley mountain folds and which are valley folds.)

1 Having drawn the diagram, cut out the shape, then fold the panels to create a square tube.

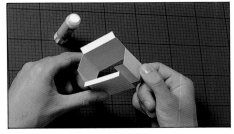

2 Glue the end tab so that the box can stand square over the gutter crease. Fold the panels to secure the shape.

3 Glue the underside of the remaining tabs. Pull the tabs apart to stretch the tube square, then lower it onto a backing sheet in such a way that the two creases running down the middle of the tube line up *exactly* with the gutter crease. Press the glued tabs onto the backing sheet.

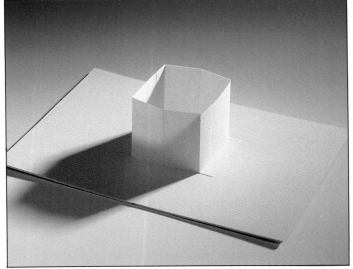

RIGHT The box can be any proportion, but should not be more than one-and-a-half times higher than its width across the gutter crease. If too tall, the sides begin to collapse inwards and look ungainly.

TRUCK
height 10 cm (4 in)
Though essentially a pop-up made using the Square-on Box technique, this construction could also perhaps have been described as being made using the Floating Layers technique; just visible are vertical supports rising from the gutter crease to the top surfaces of the truck. Note the exhaust pipes, wing mirrors and recessed wheels made using the Cut Away technique. The surface was rendered with marker pens.

Square-on Box Variations

I (LEFT) The extra panels are used here to create a hexagonal (six-sided) box. *II (CENTRE)* The two panels open to create an excellent cylinder. This shape always makes an impression as curves are rare in pop-ups. The cylinder cannot be very tall if it is to open fully. *III (RIGHT)* This is a solid box. The support beneath the lid is not essential, but it helps make the lid lie flat, which it would not do otherwise.

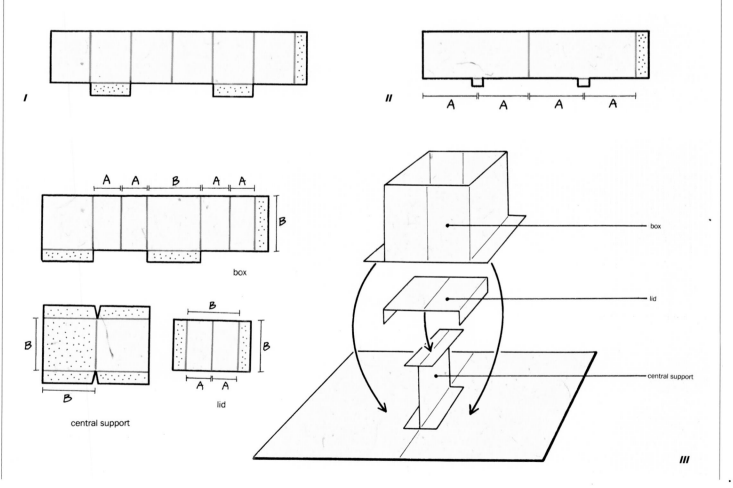

I

II

A   A   A   A

A   A   B   A   A

B

box

B   B

B   B

B   B

A   A

B

central support

lid

box

lid

central support

III

Cylinder

This unusual technique is one of the very few which creates a curved pop-up. The construction is relatively complex and must be made very precisely for the effect to work, but the results are well worth the effort. The construction has no significant variations, so no exercises are included with this technique.

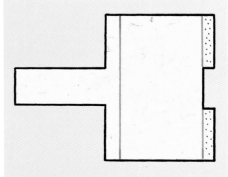

Cut out the shape of the cylinder, as shown. The length of the arm is not critical, although it is always better to overestimate its length than under-estimate; the excess can be cut off later.

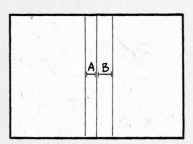

Using a pencil, draw a line down the centre of the backing sheet. Then draw two lines parallel to the first. Note that **A** is closer to the centre line than **B**. This is important.

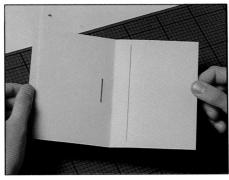

1 Having drawn up the backing sheet, fold
.. the gutter crease and cut a slot along the left-hand line (**A**), a little larger than the width of the cylinder arm.

2 Fold over the tabs on the cylinder and
.. apply glue to them.

3 Fix the glued tabs to the backing sheet
.. along the right-hand vertical line, having first folded the strap on the cylinder under the cylinder block and *between* the glued tabs, so that it protrudes to the left, as shown.

4 Fold the backing sheet in half. Tuck the
.. protruding strap through the slot.

5 Secure the arm with a piece of masking or
.. sticky tape.

KIOSQUE AU JARDIN
height 20 cm (8 in)

ABOVE *This charming design, made by laminating colour photocopies of original artwork onto card (cardboard), uses the basic Cylinder technique, except that the pull tab is pushed through a slot, to continue behind the kiosk attendant, emerging through another slot and connecting with the right-hand edge of the cylinder. In this way, the artwork inside the kiosk is uninterrupted by the tab.*

LEFT As the card is opened, the arm pulls the flat piece of card (cardboard) up into a cylinder.

Trellises

This is the only technique not to be powered by the gutter crease on a backing sheet. Indeed, it does not require a backing sheet at all, because it can be pressed into shape by hand. It is a truly sculptural form, presenting the pop-up as a free-standing object in its own right.

The Trellises technique is highly adaptable. The only constant factor is that when erected and viewed from above, the slats must form a series of 90-degree intersections. If they do not cross at right angles the construction will not flatten. Therefore, the distances between the slits must be measured precisely.

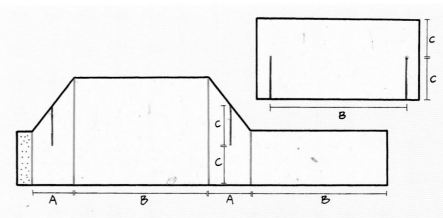

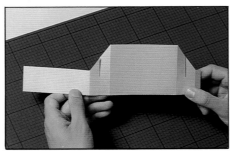

On two pieces of stiff paper and using a pencil, draw the diagrams, carefully noting each of the measurements.

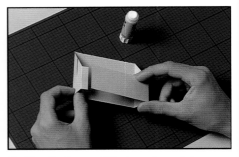

(Coloured lines have been used in this example to show which lines are for cutting and which are for folding.)

1 Having drawn the diagrams, cut out the two shapes.

2 Glue the larger of the two pieces into a rectangular tube.

3 Interlock the smaller piece into the larger using the slits.

LEFT The different heights of the three layers allows each to be seen.

Variations

I (LEFT) Whereas in the second variation the interlocking units create a square grid, in this example they form a series of diagonally connected boxes. Each unit can take any shape, perhaps creating the silhouette of a word across the top, or a train, or whatever you like. *II (RIGHT)* The ten identical units slot together to create a regular square grid that pushes flat. The units need not be identical, and they can be of any shape and interlock in an irregular pattern, providing that all the units interlock at 90 degrees when three-dimensional.

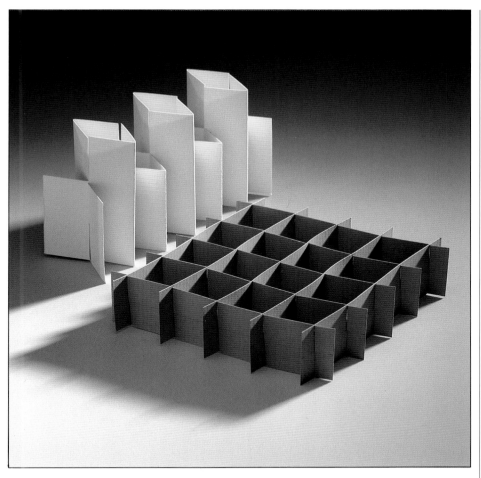

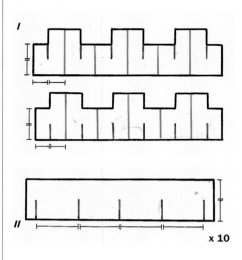

x 10

CHESS GAME
height
12 cm (4¾ in)
Eighteen identical strips of card (cardboard) slot together without glue, to create a chessboard using the Trellis technique. The chess pieces slot onto the strips and can be moved about as in an ordinary game; they stay attached to the board when it is collapsed.

Pivots

Of all the pop-up techniques, Pivots are the most entertaining because they swivel as the gutter crease is opened. They are often used in a humorous context.

Pivots are fun and easy to make but attention must be paid to the shape, length, and position of the long arm: a little carelessness will cause it to jam or crease.

DARTBOARD
height 23 cm (9 in)
The pop-up darts stand away from the dartboard using a simple pivot, but the design is still interesting because of the careful rendering of the eye-catching board, achieved with coloured pencils, gouache and chalk. A pop-up need not be technically advanced to be memorable; the illustration can be just as important.

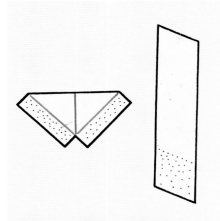

Following the diagrams, cut out a triangular tab and pivot. Fold the tab, creating one valley and two mountain creases.

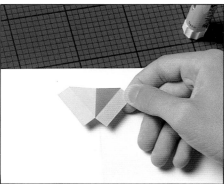

1 Glue the tab to the gutter crease, ensuring the central mountain fold and the gutter crease are exactly in line.

2 The long arm, which is to pivot, will do so with the greatest sweep if it is glued to one face of the triangular tab so that it rises perpendicularly away from the crease at the bottom of the face.

OPPOSITE BELOW The Pivot technique can work on any crease (valley or mountain). It will work better if the opening crease opens from 0 to 180 degrees, and if the triangular tab lies almost flat across a crease.

Pivots Variations

(I) Note that the pivot could be repeated at the bottom end of the mountain crease and that other pivots could be placed across the valley creases.

(II) Note how the flap hides the arm.

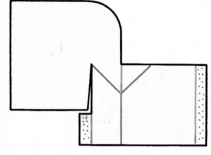

Make a horizontal Asymmetric Mountain Step form (*see* **page 49**), but add to it the "V"-shaped creased triangle, which is extended to create a large pivoting arm. Glue the step across the gutter crease. When the backing sheet is closed the arm will swivel to lie vertically.

I

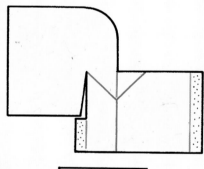

Variation I has the arm in view all the time, but if you add a large flap, stuck to the step, it will hide the arm when the card is closed, allowing it to swivel amusingly into view as it is opened.

II

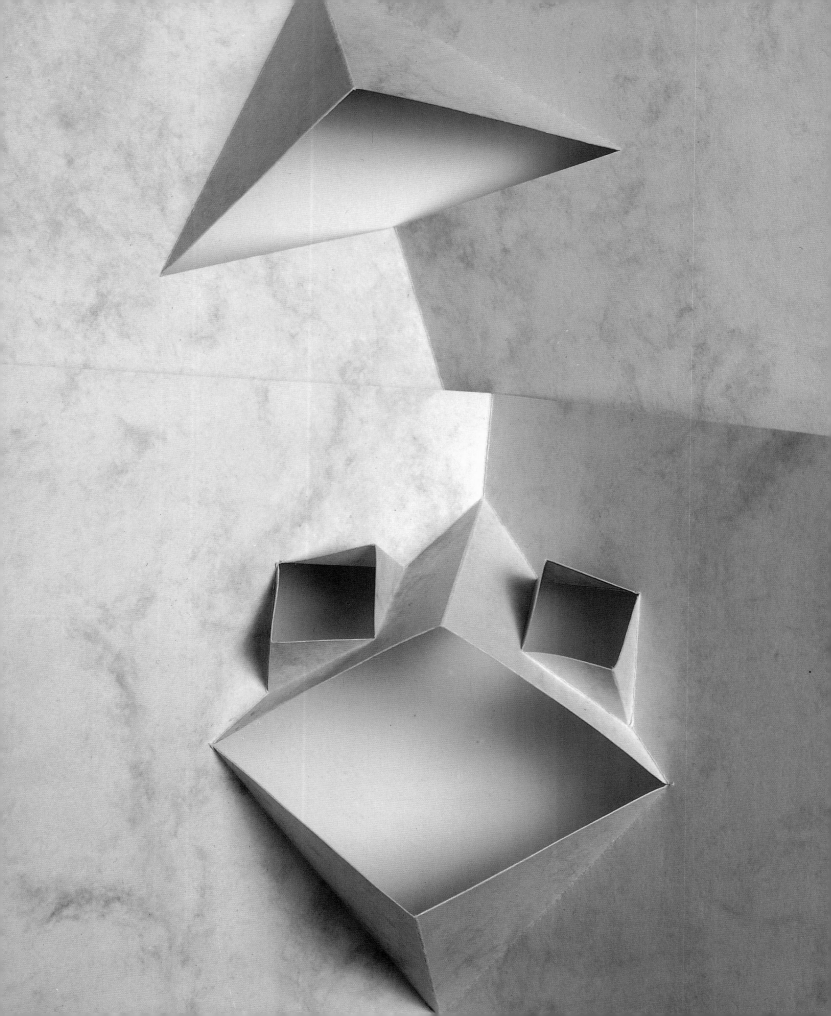

Design

Having mastered the techniques in the previous section, you should now be able to design your own pop-ups. Do not feel restricted to using the heart templates in the book; adapt your designs, and other shapes, for use as pop-us, and take inspiration from the Gallery.

How to Design Your Own Pop-ups

The preceding technical chapters explained the principles of different pop-up mechanisms, and the card designs showed how they could be used to create original pop-ups. The next stage is to begin to design your own pop-ups, for here lies the true pleasure of the art which no amount of exercise copying could ever equal.

It is important to have first understood the principles of the techniques – not all of them perhaps, but clearly the more knowledge you have, the easier it will be to overcome any design problems that arise (and they will arise!). It is better to have learned, say, all the one-piece or all the multi-piece techniques than to have learned a random selection, as this will make you proficient in at least one major technical area.

What you design is obviously a matter of your personal choice: a greetings card, invitation, business card, leaflet, mail shot, table ornament . . . The subject matter of the design will probably precede any technical considerations. Once this is determined, you can then decide which technique will best suit your subject, your technical skills and perhaps even your budget.

To help you decide, and to demonstrate how almost any subject matter can be married to almost any technique, this chapter uses the Valentine heart in every example. The heart could equally have been a birthday cake, a Christmas tree, a face, numerals or anything else, but the simplicity of the heart helps draw attention to the techniques and away from any possible distractions, such as an unnecessarily complex outline or form, which could confuse rather than clarify. The Double Hearts and the Heart with Arrow designs show how one form can be combined with another to create more intricate multiple-subject structures.

Of course this catalogue is by no means complete – it never could be – but it should go a long way towards demonstrating how adaptable pop-up techniques are for *any* subject matter, and how surprisingly easy it is to create an original design. It should also give you the confidence to begin designing your own pop-ups.

OPPOSITE
WATERFALLS OF THE SIERRA NEVADA
box dimensions 40 x 20 x 8 cm
(15¾ x 8 x 3 in)
This concertina pop-up stands some 6 m (6½ yd) tall when suspended. Its zig-zag shape is held in place by running threads which pull taut when the pop-up is suspended; without them they would flatten. The pop-up will collapse flat and is housed in the box seen beneath it, though the box is not part of the display. This beautiful pop-up is decorated with watercolour, gold pen, cotton and reflective foil.

Single Hearts

The designs in this section show how a single subject can be made to pop up using a wide variety of techniques, both one-piece and multi-piece. The specific techniques used here and the forms generated relate exclusively to the shape of a heart. However, with a little imagination, the same techniques can be adapted in form to represent any other subject of your choice. The heart templates shown in this chapter can be enlarged but the different elements of the designs must remain in proportion to each other.

Design One

This is arguably the simplest of all pop-up hearts and uses the Shape of Slit technique (*see* **page 26**). Note how by doubling over the paper at the back, the construction becomes surprisingly sturdy, even though it is made from paper not card (cardboard). Use a medium-weight paper; the paper used in this project has a marble-effect pattern.

1 Fold a sheet of paper in half and press the
.. gutter crease firmly.

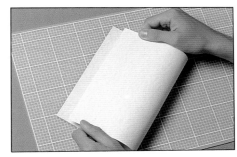

2 Fold it in half again, then unfold it
.. completely.

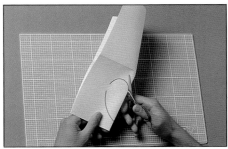

3 Fold the paper in half, in the same way
.. that you did for step 1. Then draw a half-heart shape from the gutter crease. Cut through both layers of paper, but leave a small part uncut.

4 This photograph shows the cut out heart.
.. Be careful not to tear the small join.

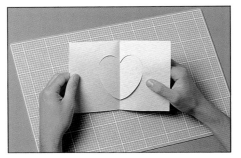

5 Unfold the paper, then fold it along the
.. central horizontal line, so that the heart is in the front.

6 Form the pop-up by lifting the heart up and
.. creating a mountain fold down the centre of the gutter crease.

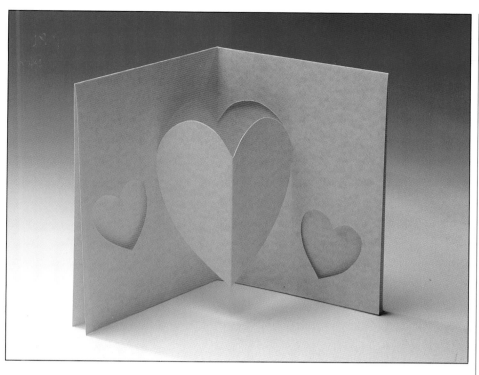

7 Close the card and reinforce all the creases by pressing firmly.

The simplicity of the design has great appeal. In this instance two hearts have been cut out of the front layer as well.

Design Two

In this version, using the Asymmetric Mountain technique (*see* **page 49**), the strap to the left of the heart must be neither too thick, nor too thin. If too thick, the crease connecting it to the heart will flatten the edge of the heart; if too thin, it will be weak. Experiment with different thicknesses. Use thick paper or thin card (cardboard). This card was decorated using oil pastel over the heart and gouache to enhance the marble-effect.

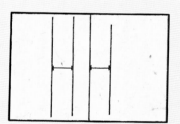

Draw a line down the middle of the paper, then add three vertical lines so that the measurements between the lines are exactly equal, as shown.

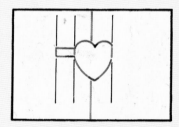

Draw a heart and tab using the vertical lines as positional guides, and note that the heart is off-centre. Erase the excess lines, such as the gutter crease inside the heart, then cut and crease following the colour coding.

The card looks at its best when viewed, not symmetrically, but a little to one side so that the heart is square-on.

Design Three

This card is similar to the card in design two, but incorporates the Cut Away technique (*see* **page 58**) so that the heart pierces the plane of the card. Use thick paper or thin card (cardboard). This card was decorated using gouache sprayed onto the surface, with a red, overpainted heart.

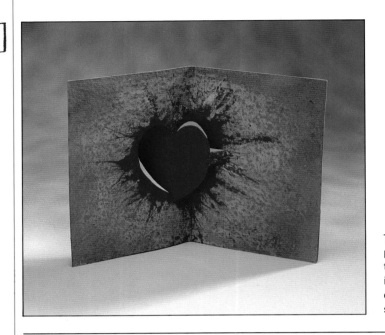

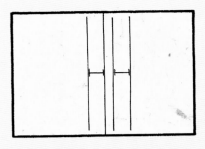

Mark a line down the middle of the card, then add three more vertical lines.

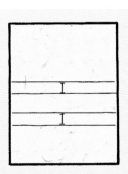

Draw the heart-like shape and tab. Note that the two halves of the heart do not meet square-on. Erase the central part of the gutter crease, then cut and crease, following the colour coding.

The piercing of the plane of the card by the heart creates an intriguing, three-dimensional structure.

Design Four

The Cut Away technique (*see* **page 58**) is used here to create a bold silhouette of the heart, although some drawing is necessary to complete the outline. In this example, the card was decorated using a red marker pen on white card (cardboard), but you can use any thick paper or thin card.

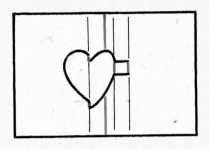

Mark a line across the centre of the paper, then add three horizontal lines so that the distances between each pair of lines is exactly equal.

Draw the design. Erase all excess lines, then cut and crease to form the pop-up, following the colour coding.

The simple technique of throwing a shape up from a basic step form is effective and extremely adaptable.

Design Five

This project is similar to design four. The difference is that the heart is now turned sideways with a step on each side. Use thick paper or thin card (cardboard). This example uses a red matt card, against a pearl blue one.

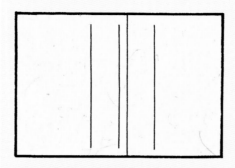

Draw a line down the middle of the card. Add the vertical lines so that the distances indicated are exactly equal.

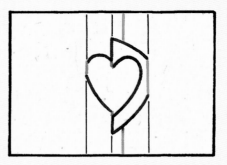

Draw the design as shown, taking care to match up each part of the shape with the correct vertical line. The two halves of the heart are not totally aligned. Erase all excess lines, then cut and crease to form the pop-up, following the colour codes.

The curious cuts and creases pattern of this construction creates an original and unexpected pop-up form.

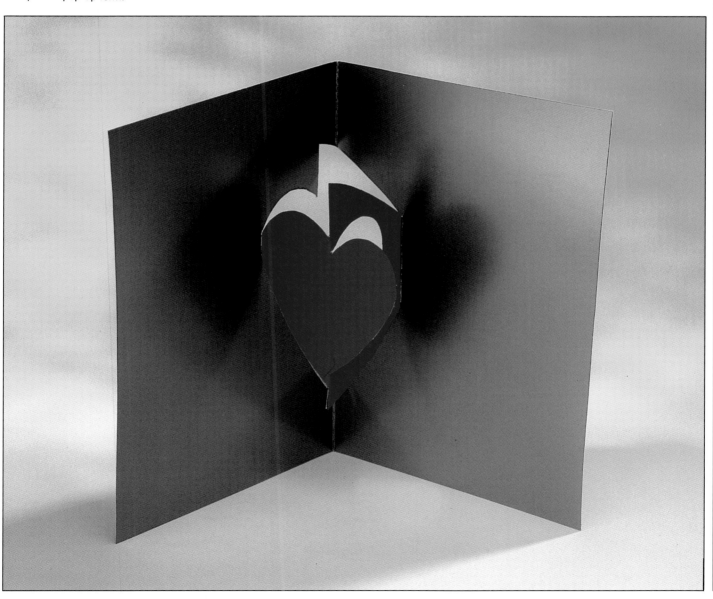

Design Six

Sometimes, as with this project, extra creases are needed to create a pop-up. By using this technique, the heart is made to stand away from the backing sheet, using a connecting stem which acts as a multi-piece Horizontal "V" (*see* **page 70**).
Note too, how this relatively complex structure is made from just one slit. Use thin card (cardboard), possibly of different colours.

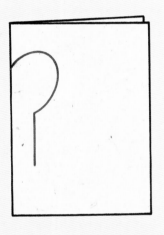

Fold the card in half, and draw the half heart and stem design.

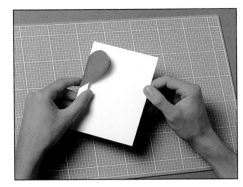

1 Using a craft knife, carefully cut out the
.. heart and stem.

2 Form two valley creases at the base of the
.. stem by folding backwards and forwards.

3 Unfold the card and lift up the heart and
.. stem; note the valley creases.

4 Crease the "V"-shaped fold at the top of
.. the stem so that the heart swivels to the horizontal. Note how the crease down the centre of the heart becomes a valley.

5 Complete the pop-up by folding down the
.. edges of the backing sheet.

OPPOSITE Note how the long creases down the edges of the card hold the card in a shallow "V"-shape, using the Horizontal "V" technique which enables the pop-up to keep its shape.

AQUARIUM
height
27 cm (10½ in)
ABOVE *This large, dense pop-up consists entirely of parallel layers made out of reflective and coloured cards (cardboard), using the Horizontal "V" technique. Fish and plant shapes have been cut to create an intriguing visible/ invisible effect, best appreciated by moving around the pop-up.*

Design Seven

Like the first project, this construction is also very basic, though no less effective for that. It uses the Asymmetric Mountain technique (*see* **page 49**). For designs other than the heart, look for suitable places to connect the tabs to the subject around its perimeter. Use thick paper or thin card (cardboard).

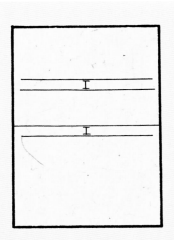

Mark a line across the middle of the card, then add the horizontal lines so that the distances indicated are exactly equal, as shown.

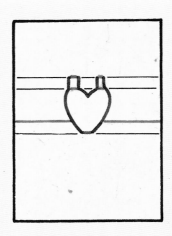

Draw the heart and tabs, and erase all excess lines. Cut and crease the pop-up, following the colour coding.

In a simple pop-up such as this, much of the success of the design depends on the choice of paper or card (cardboard) and, if used, any surface decoration. This card was decorated with a gold marker pen.

Design Eight

This is the most complex project in the chapter, but made easier because all the basic measurements are the same. It uses the Multi Slit technique (*see* **page 60**). To aid accuracy, it may be advisable to fix squared paper to the back of the card, and to cut and crease on that side. Use thick paper.

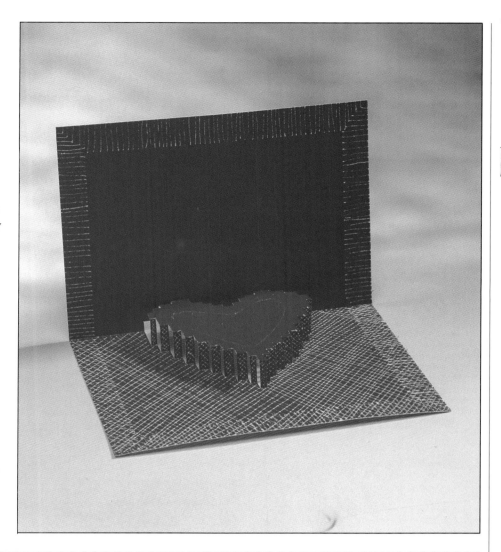

The design must be made with great accuracy if it is to look good, but the extra care will be well rewarded! This card was decorated by scratching through a coated card (cardboard) with a needle, to reveal the white beneath.

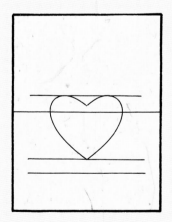

Draw a line across the middle of the paper, then add three horizontal lines so that the distances indicated are exactly equal. Draw a basic heart shape.

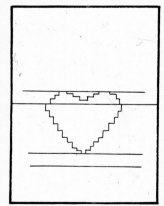

Using the original drawing as a guide, draw a "stepped" heart, taking care to ensure that the steps are symmetrical.

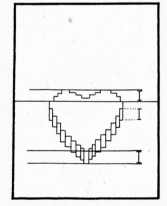

Then mark a series of vertical lines all the same length as the measurement indicated.

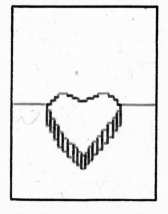

Erase all excess lines, then cut and crease the pop-up, following the colour coding.

Design Nine

Here is the simplest multi-piece heart, using the Horizontal "V" technique (*see* **page** 70) and consisting of a heart shape with two glue tabs that hold it onto the backing sheet. Use thick paper for the pop-up and sturdy card (cardboard) for the backing sheet, possibly of different colours.

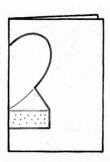

Fold a sheet of paper in half. Draw the heart design, then cut it out, following the colour coding.

Note that the angle of the "V" can change from being almost a straight line perpendicularly across the gutter crease, to being almost closed up along the gutter crease. In this example, the central area of the "Vs" has been cut out.

Unfold the paper. Crease across the bottom of the sheet to create the tabs. Follow the procedure described in the Horizontal "V" techniques (*see* **page 70**), to glue the tabs accurately to the backing sheet.

Design Ten

This is similar to design nine, but the crease down the centre of the heart has been removed, so that the heart becomes flat and stands at an angle to the gutter crease. Use thick paper for the pop-up and sturdy card (cardboard) for the backing sheet.

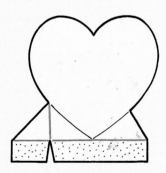

Draw the design on a sheet of thick paper, then cut it out. Follow the procedures described in the Horizontal "V" techniques (*see* **page 70**), to glue the tabs accurately to the backing sheet.

The effect is most attractive and an interesting alternative to the conventional Horizontal "V" design described in project nine.

COMIC BOOK FIGURE
height 14 cm (5½ in)
Though making very simple use of the Horizontal "V" technique (there is a crease down the figure's left leg, above the gutter crease), the highly decorated surfaces and the careful drawing ensure that the construction has great impact.

Design Eleven

Here, the heart is lifted away from the backing sheet by means of a vertical support. The result is similar to that of the one-piece construction in project six, but by using two pieces the support can be made to disappear underneath the heart to enhance the "floating" effect. Use thick paper for the pop-up and sturdy card (cardboard) for the backing sheet.

1. Then glue the support to the backing sheet, following the procedure described in the Horizontal "V" techniques section (*see* **page 70**). Form the "V" crease, as shown, swivelling the top section of the support to the horizontal.

2. Glue the heart to the top of the support, matching the "V" crease of the support exactly with the "V" crease of the heart.

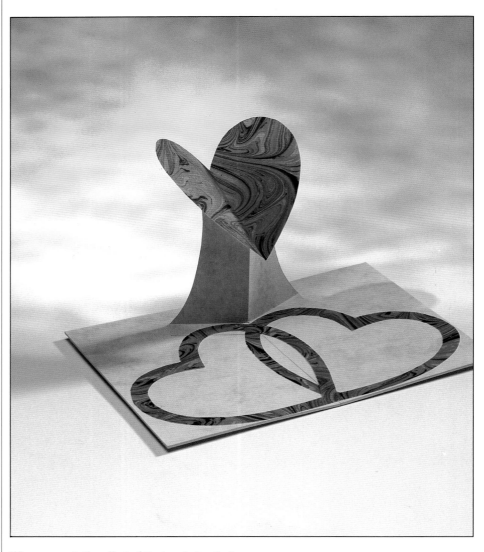

When opened, the effect of the heart standing right away from the backing sheet can be very dramatic. Note that the taller the support becomes, the less power it will have to open the heart fully.

Cut out a heart shape of generous width (the wider it is, the wider the support can be, and the better the mechanism will work).

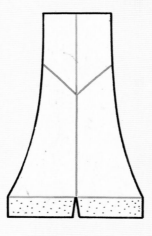

Using the template as a guide, cut out the support. Note that its width should be a little less than the width of the heart, so as not to be seen. Also, note the shallow "V" crease. Form the creases, following the colour coding on the template.

Design Twelve

Using exercise V of the Horizontal "V" techniques (*see* **page 73**), the heart swivels over the top edge of the backing sheet when it is opened. Note that the pop-up shape is not a complete heart, but only two thirds. This is to create enough width for the tabs. The result is that the rest of the heart has to be drawn onto the backing sheet. Use thick paper for the pop-up and sturdy card (cardboard) for the backing sheet. This card was effectively decorated by airbrushing.

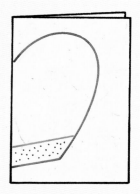

Fold a thick sheet of paper in half, then draw the heart design. Cut out the shape, including the tabs, and then fold it out flat.

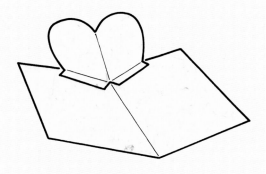

Crease the tabs, creating valley folds, and then glue the shape to the backing sheet, following the procedure described in the Horizontal "V" techniques section (*see* **page 70**).

Note how the pop-up swivels into the card as it is closed. The bottom part of the heart is drawn on the backing sheet.

Design Thirteen

The Floating Layers technique (*see* **page 74**) is an excellent way to lift a shape away from the backing sheet. It is more complex than the technique used in project eleven, but the result is more reliable. Use thick paper for the pop-up and sturdy card (cardboard) for the backing sheet.

Using the template as a guide, cut out a heart from thick paper.

Make three supports as described in the Floating Layers technique.

1 Glue the three supports to the backing sheet.

2 Finally, glue the heart into position on top.

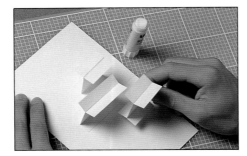

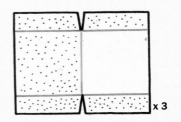

If an asymmetrical composition is preferred, the heart may be creased not down the middle, but along any other line.

COMPUTER BROCHURE
height 14 cm (5½ in)

Created as a project piece by a student of Graphic Design, this piece explores how a pop-up could be used to give visual impact to an otherwise conventional sales brochure. The structure is made using the Floating

Layers technique, though unusually, the gutter crease lies beneath the screen, so the left-hand half of the structure has virtually been removed, replaced by a supporting prop (out of sight to the camera).

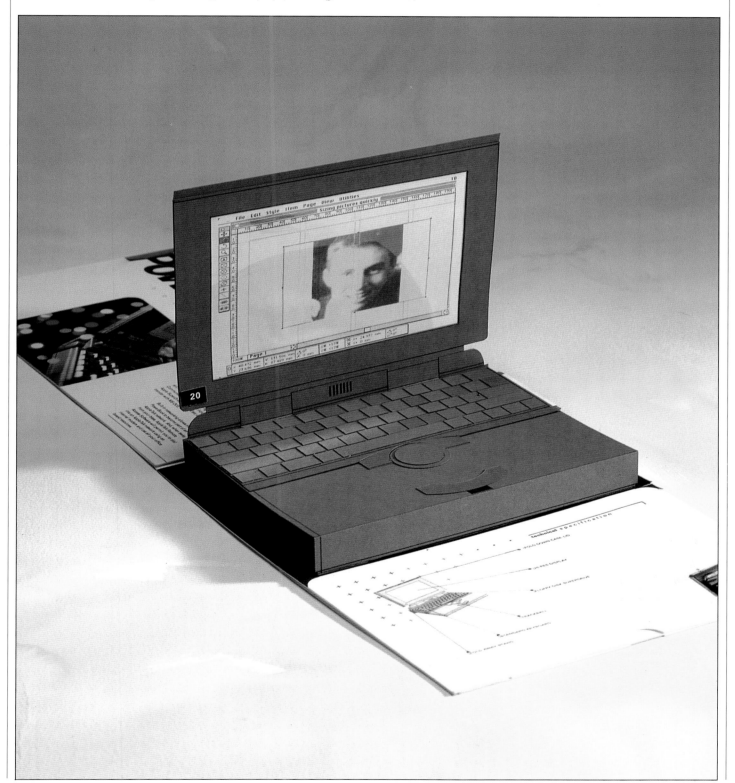

Design Fourteen

This project is another of the simplest. The Scenery Flats technique (*see* **page 78**) is a quick and easy way to create a support for any pop-up shape. Pop-up "purists" may wish to cut the support from the backing sheet, rather than gluing a separate support to the backing sheet. Use thick paper for the heart and support, and sturdy card (cardboard) for the backing sheet.

The Scenery Flats technique is versatile, but if the supporting tabs are too long the heart will stand well away from the gutter crease, and fall even further away when the card is closed up. If this is the case, the card will have to be unnecessarily deep to accommodate the falling heart.

Cut out a heart and a support from a sheet of thick paper; note the glue tabs on the support.

Glue the support to the backing sheet so that the distances indicated are measured and equal. Then glue the heart to one of the faces.

Design Fifteen

The Pivot technique (*see* **page 92**) will always bring a little humour to any greetings card: the swivelling of the pivot as the card opens creates unexpected movement, which can be used to good effect, as with the "Karate Kick" opposite. Use thick paper for the heart and support, and sturdy card (cardboard) for the backing sheet. This example was made using decorative papers laminated onto card.

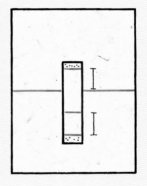

Using the template as a guide, cut out a heart and support.

1 Crease the support, following the mountain and valley folds shown on the template. Glue the support flat to the backing sheet, using the method described in the Horizontal "V" techniques section (*see* **page 70**).

KARATE KICK
height
24 cm (9½ in)
This is a near-identical reworking of exercise II of the Pivot technique. As the card is opened, the right leg emerges from behind the left leg and the left forearm from behind the head. Both pivot to the horizontal to mimic accurately a karate movement. The card is best appreciated while it is being opened and closed.

2 Glue the heart to one face of the support.
Experiment with the angles to achieve
the maximum swivel when the card is opened.

Note that the flatter the support is stuck to the
backing sheet, the flatter the heart will lie.

Double Hearts

The theme of two hearts shows how a design with two separate elements can be made to pop up using a variety of different techniques. These techniques can be adapted to other pop-ups in which the two or more elements are not identical as they are here. Two hearts are of course a little more complex to make than one, so extra care must be taken when measuring and assembling.

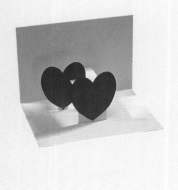

Design One

The Generations technique (*see* **page 55**) can create extremely complex pop-up forms, but great care must be taken to ensure that when foreground forms are cut away from background forms, the latter do not become abstracted by losing too much of their shape. This is why the positioning of the smaller heart on the larger must be done with accuracy. Use thin card (cardboard) for the project. This card was decorated using felt-tipped pens.

OPPOSITE RIGHT If a solid back is preferred, the card can be made with an extra layer to the rear, as described in the first Single Heart design.

Design Two

In this project the Cut Away intertwining of the two hearts over the gutter crease creates a curious but attractive effect. Note how the crease formed where the hearts meet is not a mountain, as might be expected, but a valley. Use thin card (cardboard). The card shown in this example was decorated using an airbrush, with separate masks for the hearts and clouds.

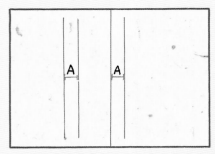

Mark a line down the middle of the card, then add three vertical lines so that the distances **A** indicated are exactly equal.

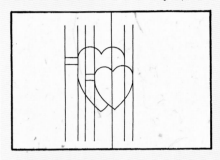

Draw the two hearts and tabs carefully so that each part of the design is aligned to the correct vertical line.

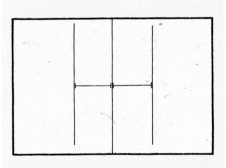

Draw a line down the middle of the card, then add two lines equidistant from the central one.

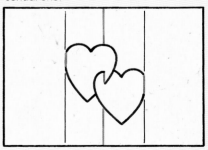

Draw the two hearts, noting how they fit together, and how they sit on the vertical lines. Erase all excess lines, then cut and crease, following the colour coding.

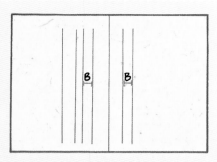

Similarly, mark three more lines, this time making sure that distances **B** are exactly equal.

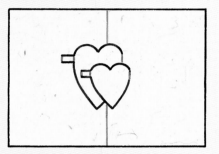

Erase all excess lines, then carefully cut and crease the pop-up, following the colour coding.

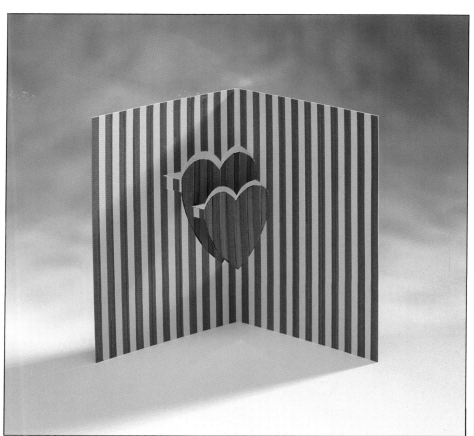

The Cut Away technique joining the two hearts is used here to great effect. Careful drawing of the hearts will contribute much to the success of the project.

Design Three

Cards that use the Generations technique (*see* **page 55**) can be difficult to make if the tabs for the second generation pop-up are of different lengths, but careful planning will ensure that such constructions can be made with the minimum of problems. Use thin card (cardboard) and follow the instructions with particular care.

In some circumstances, the long tab connecting the second generation heart to the back of the card can be completely removed, so that the heart is connected only to the first generation heart. However, here, two tabs have been used as they create a stronger pop-up.

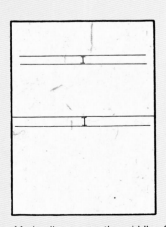

Mark a line across the middle of the card, and then add three horizontal lines, ensuring that the distances indicated are exactly equal.

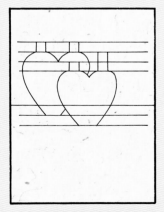

Similarly, add three more lines.

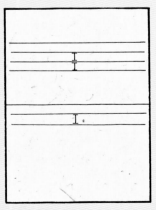

Draw the two hearts and tabs, noting the long tab to the right.

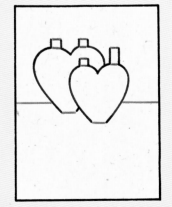

Rub out all the excess lines, then cut and crease the card to form the pop-up, following the colour codes.

Design Four

This design is similar to the fourth Single Heart project, but with the addition of the Asymmetric Angles technique (*see* **page 52**) which twists the pop-up off-square. Measure the angles carefully. Use thin card (cardboard), and you will also need a protractor. This card was decorated with pastels.

Note that any of the one-piece constructions in this chapter which are parallel to the gutter crease can be adapted to use the Asymmetric Angle technique.

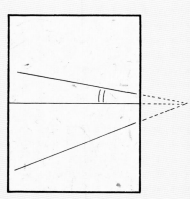

Draw a line across the middle of the card. Imagine a focal point (**x**) off the area of the sheet. Draw two sloping lines to meet at **x**. Measure the smaller angle.

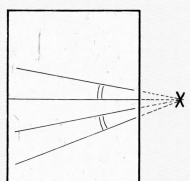

Draw a third sloping line to **x** so that the two indicated angles are equal.

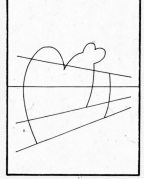

Draw the two hearts, making sure they are properly aligned with the straight lines.

Erase all excess lines, then cut and crease the pop-up, following the colour coding.

Design Five

A simple shape, such as a heart, is ideal for a Generations card in which each successive generation is built inside the previous one to create an intriguing "negative/positive" effect. Use thin card (cardboard). This design was decorated by laminating coloured papers onto card.

The concentric effect can be continued if more hearts are formed. A coloured sheet of card placed behind the hearts will make the negative (empty) heart shapes more visible.

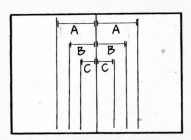

Draw a line down the middle of the card. Using this line, the gutter crease, as a common reference, draw three parallel sets of lines, as shown.

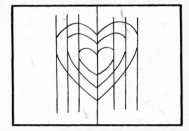

Use the vertical lines as a guide to locate the outlines of three hearts.

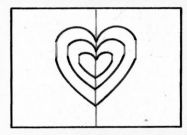

Rub out all the excess lines, then cut and crease the pop-up, following the colour codes.

Design Six

The Wings technique (*see* **page 66**) is ideal for joining together multiple subjects. Two hearts can be joined back-to-back to form a single three-dimensional heart or, as in this project, can be joined askew to create two linked hearts. Use thin card (cardboard).

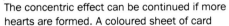

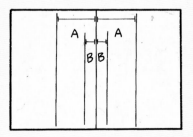

ABOVE Draw a line down the middle and two lines equidistant from it. Add two more equidistant lines further out.

ABOVE RIGHT Draw a line across the centre, then draw two hearts, as shown. In particular, note the positioning of the slits.

BELOW RIGHT Erase all excess lines, then cut and crease the pop-up, following the colour coding. Interlink the hearts, using the slits.

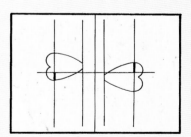

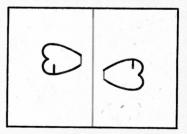

STATUE OF LIBERTY
height 32 cm (12½ in)

ABOVE *The interest in this pop-up lies not in the construction – in which mirror images of the Statue of Liberty are placed astride the gutter crease and glued together, using the Wings technique – but in the way the surface has been rendered. The surface is that of a diary, a collage of many everyday images and objects of typical American culture. By overpainting the flag, the overall effect of collage and paint is reminiscent of Jasper John's "Flag" paintings.*

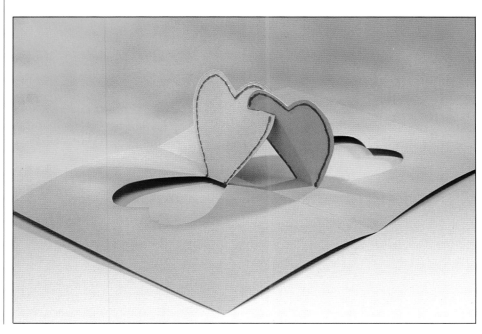

LEFT For the pop-up to work well, the positioning of the two short slits is critical.

Design Seven

Similar to the previous project, this variation has twisted the hearts through 90 degrees, so that they are connected to the backing sheet by creases along the side of the hearts, not at the bottom as before. The construction is otherwise identical and uses the Wings technique (*see* **page 66**). Use thin card (cardboard), which can be decorated in many ways; the card in this project is decorated with oil pastels.

The two hearts can be set at different levels and at different angles to each other to create any number of unusual compositions. See also page 131 for a heart pierced by an arrow made using the same technique.

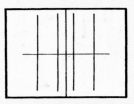

Follow the construction of design six (*see* **step 1**), then draw a horizontal line.

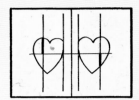

Add two hearts, noting that the position of the slits differs on each heart.

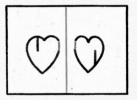

Erase all excess lines, then cut and crease the pop-up, following the colour coding. Interlock the hearts.

Design Eight

This project, and the one that follows, are similar to Double Heart projects two and seven, but have been made to stand up from a 180-degree (flat) backing sheet. Use thick paper for the pop-up and sturdy card (cardboard) for the backing sheet. In this card the centres of the hearts were cut out.

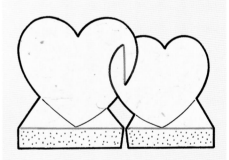

Cut out the hearts, following the templates. Note how they intertwine at the centre and how a short vertical crease forms. Glue the shape to the backing sheet, following the procedure described in the Horizontal "V" techniques section (*see* **page 70**).

The wide base to each heart is necessary to "power" the heart upright when the card is opened. If they had narrow bases, the hearts would fall weakly inwards when the card was opened.

Design Nine

Similar to the previous two projects, this variation demonstrates the adaptability of pop-up techniques. There is always more than one way to achieve the same effect, a fact which is sometimes difficult for the novice to appreciate. Use thick paper for the pop-up and sturdy card (cardboard) for the backing sheet. This spectacular example uses embossed gold foil, laminated with red paper and splattered with gouache.

The two slits will lock the hearts together well, but they must be accurately cut. If they need strengthening, add a piece of sticky tape.

Cut out two heart shapes, identical but for the slits, from thick paper. Cut and crease, following the colour coding, then interlock the two slits. Glue the hearts to the backing sheet, following the procedure described in Horizontal "V" techniques (*see* **page 70**).

Design Ten

The Floating Layers technique enables pop-ups of different heights to co-habit the same gutter crease to good effect. It also enables the floating shapes to be creased at any angle, creating an interesting asymmetric relationship between the two shapes. Use thick paper for the pop-ups and sturdy card (cardboard) for the backing sheet.

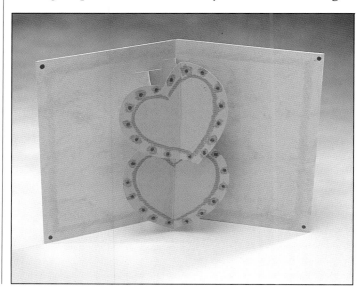

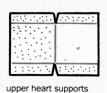

upper heart

upper heart supports

x 3

Cut out two heart shapes, following the templates. The creases can be in any position.

The overlapping of one heart over the other creates an interesting layered effect. It is not advisable to make the supports too high, as this begins to both distort the shape of the floating layer and make the structure look ungainly.

lower heart

lower heart support

x 3

Make six supports, three of one height and three of another. Glue the supports to the backing sheet and the hearts to the supports, following the procedure described in the Floating Layers technique (*see* **page 74**).

Design Eleven

The basic Scenery Flats technique seen in the fourteenth Single Heart project is adequate, but the horizontal support can also be used to support further shapes. The double heart is ideally suited to this technique. Use thick paper for the pop-ups and sturdy card (cardboard) for the backing sheet.

BELOW It is easy to make the mistake of cutting the slits in the heart and the support too long, so that when interlocked the rear heart slides too far to lie directly behind the front heart. Make the slits shorter than necessary, then elongate them if necessary.

Cut out two heart shapes, following the templates. Note that one has a glue tab and a horizontal slit at the bottom.

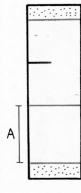

Make the horizontal support. Note that the slit and the measured distance are equal to that on the heart.

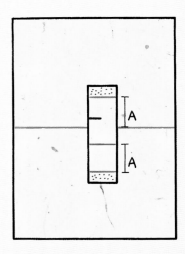

Glue the support to the backing sheet so that the measured distances are equal.

1 Interlock the heart with the slit. The two slits will slide together if the measurements have been made accurately.

2 Glue the other heart to the front of the support.

height 13 cm (5 in)
The Scenery Flats technique is used here. A rubber band is stretched diagonally from front to back to keep the structure in tension. Releasing the pressure allows the band to contract, so that the sheep automatically erects itself.

Design Twelve

If one support will enable a Scenery Flat shape to face one way, two supports pointing in opposite directions will allow two shapes to point in opposite directions. This project is a doubling of the previous project and creates an interesting effect. Use thick paper for the pop-ups and sturdy card (cardboard) for the backing sheet.

The mirroring of the two supports creates hearts that are parallel to each half of the backing sheet. This creates a structure of pleasing complexity, yet is very simple to make. Other supports can also be added.

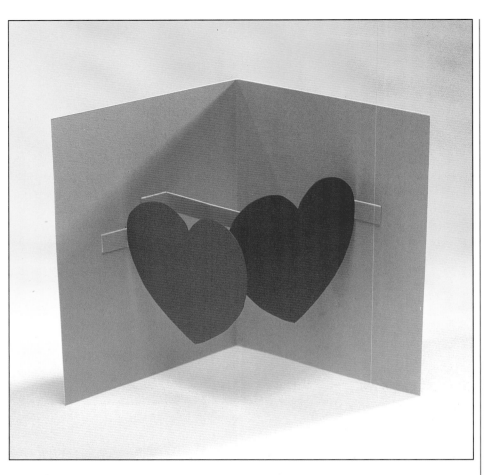

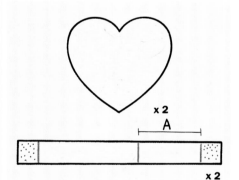

Using the templates as a guide, make two identical supports and then two identical hearts.

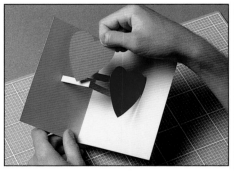

1 Glue one support across the gutter, making
▪▪ sure that the measured distances are equal. Glue down the other support but rotate it 180 degrees to the first, so that the shorter face is on the opposite side of the gutter crease to the first (*see* **figs 1** and **2**).

2 Glue the hearts to the shorter faces in
▪▪ such a way that the whole structure will fold in half and shut (*see* **fig 3**).

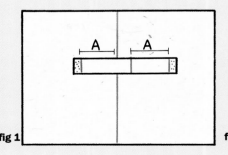

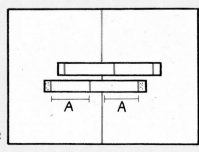

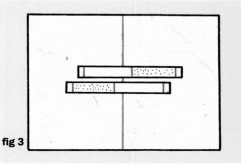

fig 1   fig 2   fig 3

Design Thirteen

Scenery flats need not be glued to supports that lie square-on to the backing sheet; they can lie at other angles, eliminating the box-like effect of the previous project. Also, one support can provide the ground for a second generation, as shown here. Use thick paper for the pop-ups and sturdy card (cardboard) for the backing sheet.

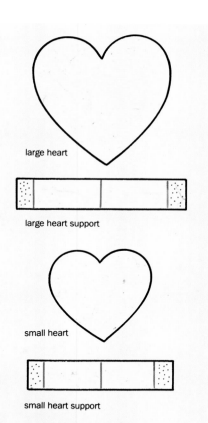

large heart

large heart support

small heart

small heart support

Using the template as a guide, make two supports. Note that one is smaller than the other. Make two hearts, one a little smaller than the other.

The technique may continue to three or four generations of supports, each built on the previous one. By changing the angle of the "V" formed by each support, the flats can lie at different angles to each other.

1 Glue the larger support to the backing sheet by positioning it symmetrically across the gutter crease.

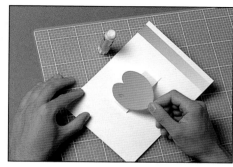

2 Glue the larger heart to one side of the support.

3 Glue the second support symmetrically to the backing sheet and the heart, as in step 2.

4 Finally, glue the second heart to the smaller support.

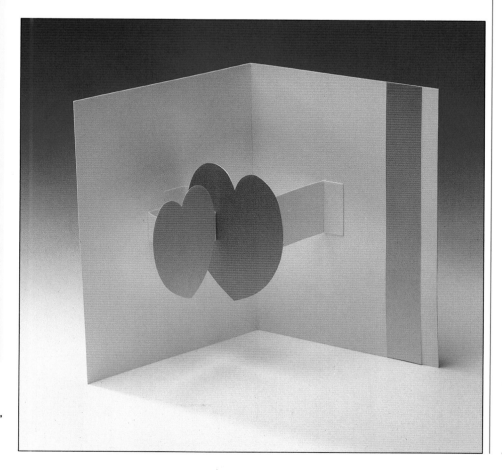

Design Fourteen

An advantage of the Straps technique (*see* **page 82**) is to remove the pop-up form from the gutter crease, to create an unexpected empty centre to the construction. The two hearts shown here are identical, but could be different. Use thick paper for the pop-ups and sturdy card (cardboard) for the backing sheet.

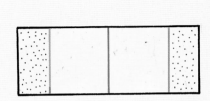

Make two hearts and a strap.

x 2

BELOW The Straps technique can be used to even more dramatic effect if the mountain crease is off-centre, creating an asymmetrical strap. The result is two pop-ups placed asymmetrically either side of the gutter crease.

1 Glue the strap symmetrically to the backing sheet, ensuring the central mountain fold is aligned to the gutter crease.

2 Then glue a heart to each end of the strap, following the procedure described in the Horizontal "V" techniques (*see* **page 70**). Two smaller hearts have been added for decoration.

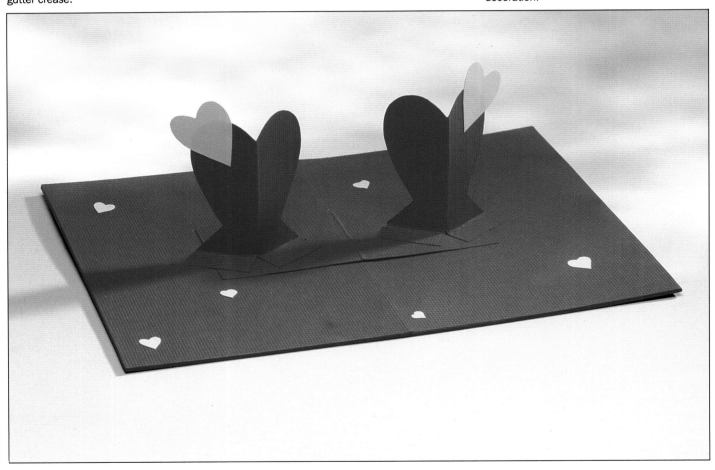

Design Fifteen

A strap need not have its creases in parallel, as in the previous project, but they may swivel to create a "V" shape, as here. This creates two pop-ups which do not point *along* the gutter crease, as before, but face each other *across* it. Use thick paper for the pop-ups and sturdy card (cardboard) for the backing sheet.

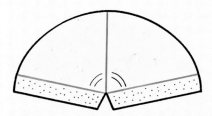
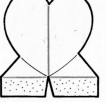

Make the strap, being careful to note the equal angles. Then make the two hearts.

x 2

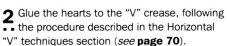

BELOW Using the Asymmetric Angles technique, the "V" creases can be made to lie asymmetrically each side of the gutter crease. The result is a bizarre non-alignment of the pop-up on the "V"

1 Glue the strap across the gutter crease, following the Straps technique shown on page 82.

2 Glue the hearts to the "V" crease, following the procedure described in the Horizontal "V" techniques section (*see* **page 70**).

Design Sixteen

The Trellis technique (*see* **page 90**) creates three-dimensional pop-ups which are not powered by a gutter crease unfolding, but which are pressed into shape. This Double Heart design has four creases which create the basic square trellis form, but it stands on only three points. The result is simple and symmetrical, yet far removed from the typical trellis "box". Use thin card (cardboard).

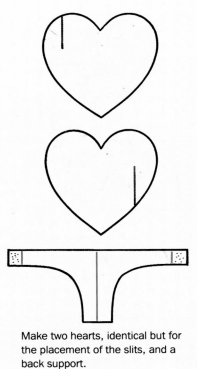

Make two hearts, identical but for the placement of the slits, and a back support.

1 Interlock the two hearts.

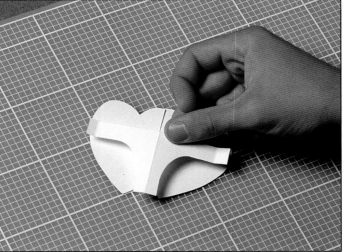

2 Glue the support to the back of the hearts, aligning the central crease on the support with the slits, ensuring that the bottom of the support is level with the bottom of the hearts. The form will push open to create a square.

PARALLO
height 10 cm (4 in)

ABOVE *Made from just three pieces of card (cardboard), which slot together without glue using the Trellis principle, this commercially available card creates a dynamic abstract form. The clever use of black and white helps to exaggerate the complexity of the structure.*

LEFT To help it stabilize, it may be necessary to place a piece of tape across the slits, at the back of the card. The back support may be replaced by two more hearts.

Hearts with Arrows

· · · · · · · · · · ·

Whereas the Double Hearts section showed how double subject pop-ups can be made when both subjects are large in area, this section shows how two subjects that are very different in shape and size can be made not only to pop-up, but also to touch (the arrow must always pierce the heart).

These new requirements necessitate a new set of technical criteria. As always, it is important to measure and assemble with care.

Design One

The Cut Away technique (*see* **page 58**) used here, creates curious "negative" shapes, such as the arrowhead in the heart. The zig-zag step in the shaft of the arrow must be minimized to reduce the stepping effect, but if the creases it forms are too short, the construction may rip. Use thin card (cardboard). This card is decorated using pastels broken to a powder and rubbed onto a marble-effect card.

To add to the effect, the arrow need not be horizontal, but could be at an angle, perhaps pointing downwards. This would still create a collapsible pop-up provided the creases remain vertical and parallel to the gutter.

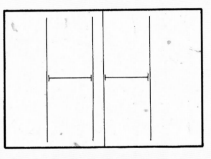

Draw a line down the middle of the card, then add three vertical lines so that the measurements indicated are equal.

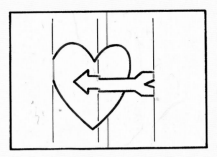

Draw the heart and arrow. Erase all excess lines, then cut and crease the pop-up, as shown.

Design Two

The major advantage of the Wings technique (*see* **page 66**) over all others, apart from its simplicity, is that double subjects are easy to make. Here, the heart and arrow are very different shapes yet can be combined with ease to pop up. Use thin card (cardboard).

The simplicity of the method has great appeal. It may be applied to many other double subjects in which the two shapes are very different.

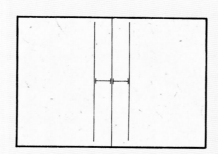

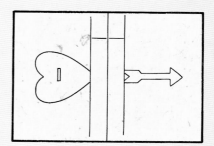

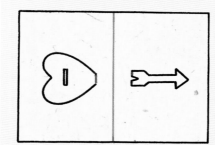

ABOVE LEFT Mark a line down the middle of a piece of card, then add two equidistant lines.

ABOVE RIGHT Draw the heart and arrow. Note the slot, which is wide enough to take the arrowhead.

LEFT Erase all excess lines, then cut and crease the pop-up. Interlock the arrow with the heart.

Design Three

The Horizontal "V" technique provides a natural angle for the arrow to pass through the heart, the heart being glued to one arm of the "V", the arrow to the other. Use thick paper for the pop-up and sturdy card (cardboard) for the backing sheet.

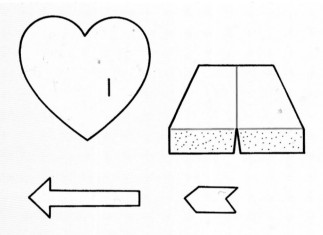

Cut out the heart, support, arrow and flight. Glue the support to the backing sheet, following the procedure described in the Horizontal "V" techniques section (*see* **page 70**).

1 Glue the heart to one arm of the "V". The slit must lie over the crease on the middle of the "V".

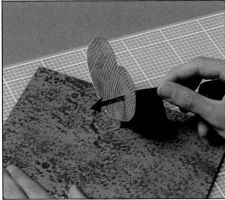

2 Push the arrow through the slit and glue it to the arm of the "V" to which the heart is *not* glued.

3 Glue the flight onto the arrow.

WINDSOR CASTLE
height 8 cm (3 in)

ABOVE *The repeated use of the Horizontal "V" technique creates a design with much charm. Note how each layer becomes taller as it recedes, ensuring that each is visible. The card was photographed from a high viewpoint to show the structure, but it is best seen from a lower angle.*

LEFT The "V"-shaped support has been used here to create an "X"- shaped pop-up. Note, particularly, how the arrow is attached to the "V": it is important to remember that a plane can be pierced to attach another plane to a support behind.

Design Four

Just as the previous project created an unexpected support for the arrow, this project does likewise: one of the supports for the floating layer comes up through the heart to create the arrow. Use thick paper for the pop-up and sturdy card (cardboard) for the backing sheet.

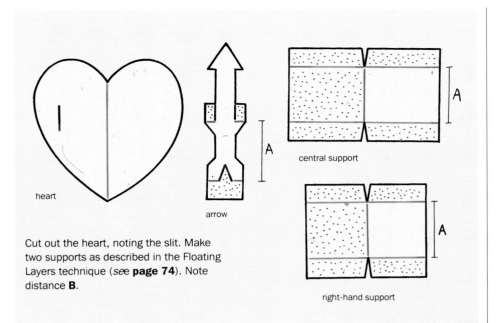

heart

arrow

central support

right-hand support

Cut out the heart, noting the slit. Make two supports as described in the Floating Layers technique (*see* **page 74**). Note distance **B**.

1 Glue the two supports to the backing
.. sheet, noting that the distance between the gutter and the right-hand support is the same as that between the crease on the heart and the slit. Glue the heart onto the supports, as described on page 74.

2 Push the arrow through the slit.
..

3 Glue it to the heart directly beneath and to
.. the backing sheet.

To add a little variety, the heart need not be glued symmetrically to the supports. See the tenth Double Heart project for a reference (page 121).

Design Five

This construction has many similarities to the second project, but is made from separate pieces to give a colourful effect. Also, the backing sheet opens to 90 degrees, instead of 180 degrees. Use thick paper for the pop-ups and sturdy card (cardboard) for the backing sheet.

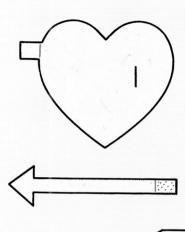

Cut out the heart, arrow and flight.

Mark a line down the middle of the card, and then add two equidistant lines.

1 Glue the heart, then the arrow, onto the backing sheet along the left-hand line.

2 Push the arrow through the slit and glue it along the right-hand line.

3 Apply glue to the flight and lay it over the glued end of the arrow, flat against the backing sheet.

When the card is opened, the two sides of the backing sheet, the heart and the arrow do not form a square as might be expected. The ability of the arrow to ride through the slit in the heart means that precise geometry is not necessary for the construction to collapse flat.

Design Six

The double Pivot technique brings an arrow and heart together in a dramatic and humorous way. Some care must be taken when constructing the card to ensure that both the arrow and the heart are hidden before the card is opened and that they come together properly when it is fully opened. Use thick paper for the pop-up and sturdy card (cardboard) for the backing sheet.

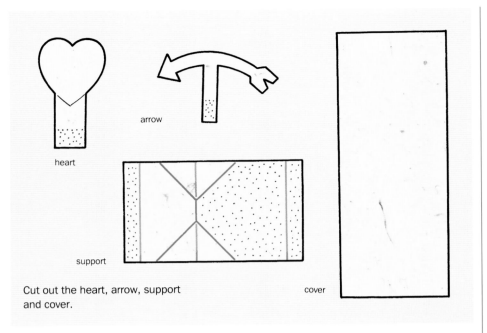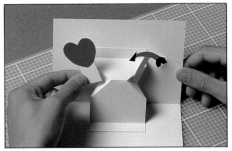

heart

arrow

support

cover

Cut out the heart, arrow, support and cover.

1 Glue the support to the backing sheet
.. (*see* **fig 1**).

2 Glue the heart and arrow to the indented
.. triangles as described in the Pivots section (*see* **page 92**).

3 Finish off the design by gluing the cover
.. over the support.

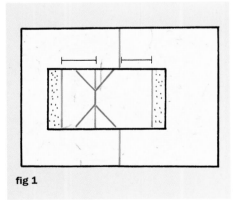

fig 1

Though fun, this card must be put together with care. Perhaps the most reliable way to construct it would be to make a rough first, so that the final, neat version would be guaranteed to work.

Design Seven

Like the sixteenth Double Heart project, this Trellis design is constructed from a creased square and stands on three points. However, instead of being based on the diagonal axis of the square, as before, this construction has the planes parallel to the side. Use thin card (cardboard).

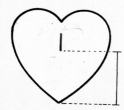

Cut out the heart. Note the critical measurement.

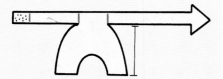

Cut out the support. Note that the crease for the arrow lies directly over the centre of the horseshoe.

The Trellis principle can be used in many ways to support a flat shape at the front. The piercing arrow seen here is not essential, but an effective bonus.

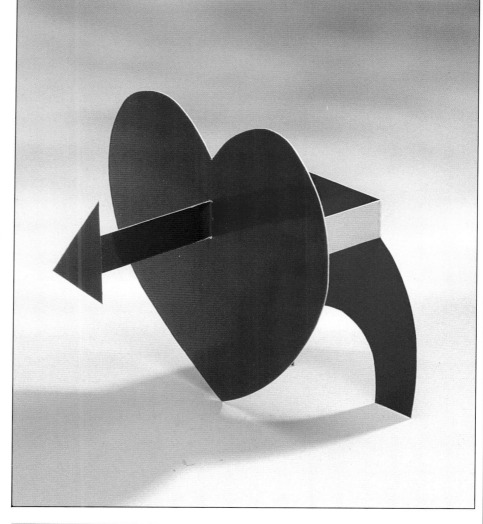

1 Apply glue to the end tab on the support, then fix it to the back of the heart near to the left-hand edge. Ensure that the bottom corner of the heart and the bottom edges of the support "legs" are level.

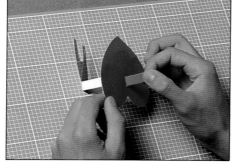

2 Push the shaft of the arrow through the slot in the heart.

3 To lock the shaft, glue on the arrowhead.

Gallery

·····················

The designs in the Gallery and in the preceding chapters form a unique collection of pop-ups. For the first time, works by professionals, students, amateurs and children are published side-by-side to reveal the art of paper-engineering as one with a previously unrecognized, but exciting, breadth of techniques, aesthetics and uses.

Most people are familiar with pop-ups in the form of books and greetings cards. The technical constraints of commercial pop-ups, such as using as few pieces and glue points as possible, and requiring easy assembly, create a

particular aesthetic which one-off, hand-made pieces need not emulate. These hand-made pop-ups are frequently constructed with greater technical freedom, often looking more like a work of art than an efficiently engineered construction, though the engineering may be just as ingenious. In the Gallery the contrast between the two becomes clear.

This collection of pop-ups also displays the importance of surface decoration. Although a designer's attention is usually focused on the engineering, the rendering of the surface is just as integral to the design, and sometimes it is more

so. Notice how some designs are highly decorated, whereas others are decorated with restraint, or sometimes not at all – the play of light and shade over a plain card can be very beautiful.

The Gallery shows the many media for which pop-ups are made today: books, greetings cards, marketing novelties, business cards, works of art, student projects, children's educational projects or simply for pleasure. The diversity of designs and the uses to which they are put has never been greater. Whatever your interest in pop-ups, this collection will inspire you.

OPPOSITE
HANGING ABSTRACT
height 36 cm (14 in)
This effective design, made out of coloured card (cardboard), is variation I of the Double Slit Cut Away technique, repeated many times on a diagonally pleated sheet of card. The repeated use of even the simplest Cut Away form (here, a semicircle), can create patterns of great beauty. Suspended from a thread and allowed to rotate, the ever-changing pattern of light and shade across the planes adds greatly to the effect.

MASKS

height 24 cm (9½ in)

Created as part of a larger series of pop-up masks by a student of Graphic Design, these technically simple pieces effectively integrate an image with text. The silver aikido mask (right) uses the Cylinder technique. The red and white African mask (below) is attached to the backing sheet on the left of the gutter crease, and slides to and fro on a strap embedded into the backing sheet, on the right.

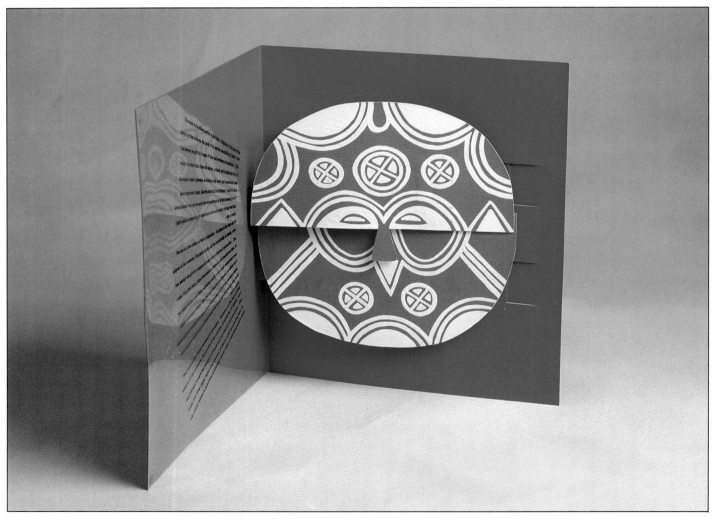

JAPANESE COURTESANS
height 4 cm (1½ in)

ABOVE *The boxed floor is exercise III of the Diagonal Box technique, subdivided in the manner of the Trellis technique. The courtesans are folded using origami techniques.*

PARTHENON
height 9 cm (3½ in)

The Square-on Box technique is used to create the basic outline of the building. Note the added white card (cardboard) spanning the gutter crease and the false yellow floor, made using the Floating Layers technique. The careful use of coloured card and pattern give visual interest to an otherwise simple construction.

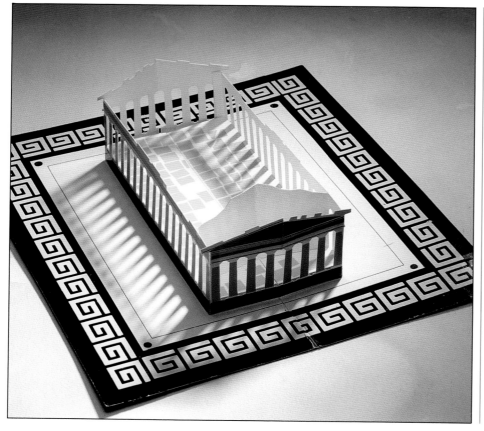

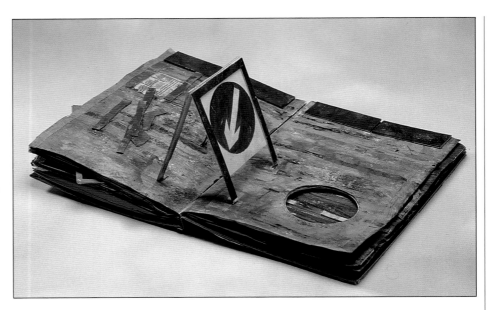

STREET FURNITURE
height 15 cm (6 in)
These two constructions form part of a pop-up book, made by a student of Graphic Design, which illustrates a short city walk. The constructions are technically simple, but they are given greater power by the vigorous rendering of the surface with thick acrylic paint, to create an unusual impasto effect that is rough to the touch.

RABBITS IN A HAT
height 10 cm (4 in)
The cylindrical box, with a separate brim, makes an excellent top hat, and the rabbits rise back-to-back from the gutter crease. The use of brightly coloured papers to create the flowers, contrasts well with the monochrome pop-up.

CRAZY CREATURES
height 9 cm (3½ in)

BELOW *This is a spread from a book of "crazy" creatures. The book, however, does not open conventionally with all the creases down the gutter, but has its creases distributed equally along the gutter, top,* outer and bottom edges. The book opens, not like a concertina, but like a series of "L" shapes and can hang like a mobile to display all the creatures simultaneously (hence the sisal).

"WONDER"
height
26 cm (10 in)

LEFT *The Wonder book was made as a student project to promote fashion designs and accessories, and features pop-ups on many of its spreads. Here, the cards are made to stand using the Horizontal "V" technique. When the pop-up erects as the spread opens, a pressure sensitive musical box begins to play a tune, which continues for as long as the page is open!*

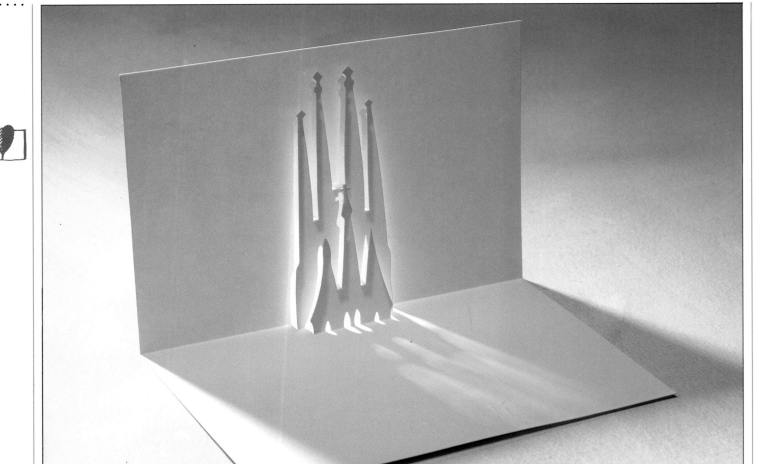

SAGRADA FAMIGLIA
height 11 cm (4¾ in)

ABOVE *The simplicity of this card demonstrates that a pop-up need not be complex to be effective. The two layers of spires are formed using the Generations technique, connected to each other and to the backing sheet by just one or two very small tabs.*

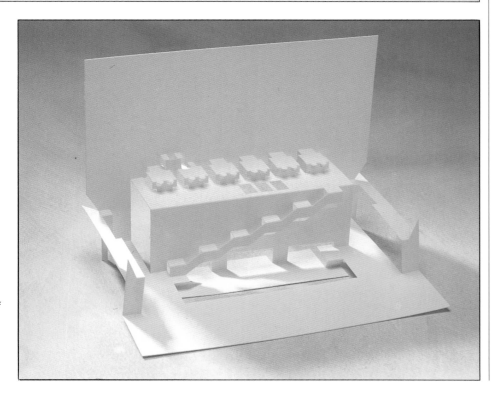

POMPIDOU CENTRE
height 11 cm (4¾ in)

RIGHT *Of particular technical interest here, is the ingenious way in which the bottom of the building descends below the backing sheet, to mimic the way in which the real building is entered from below street level. Note also the escalator construction ascending diagonally up the building.*

CHRYSANTHEMUM
height 4 cm (1½ in)

LEFT *The dense structure is achieved using the Trellis technique in an eight by eight grid of interlocking slats. No glue is used, except to hold the two slats to the backing sheet, in a similar technique to that of a Diagonal Box. Only careful measuring and cutting will ensure that a grid of this complexity will collapse flat.*

SNOWFLAKE
height 15 cm (6 in)

BELOW *The two arms of the snowflake criss-cross through the front layer of the reflective card (cardboard) and are joined to the back layer. As the card opens, the arms separate. The reflective card apparently multiplies the number of arms, to create the illusion of a three-dimensional snowflake.*

CHRISTMAS TREE
height 26 cm (10¼ in)

ABOVE *This two-piece design, made out of die-cut card (cardboard) does not pop-up automatically, but needs pressing into a three-dimensional shape from flat. The structure is essentially a diagonal box, with the two halves intertwining up the trunk. Glue tabs (out of sight at the back) hold the pieces together.*

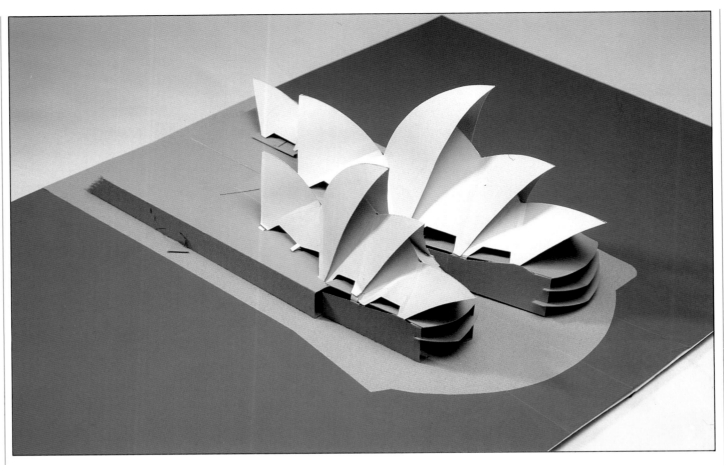

SYDNEY OPERA HOUSE
height 16 cm (6¾ in)
ABOVE *This magnificent construction, made out of colour cards (cardboard), uses the Floating Layers technique as its base, then an unusual variation on the Strap technique to collapse the two lines of roofs. The loose triangular tab at the left is attached to a thread that has to be pulled to open the small roof, at the top left.*

GOLD STAR
height 13 cm (5 in)
LEFT *Two strips of gold card (cardboard) are slotted together in a manner similar to variation II of the Trellis technique, then bent into a circle to create the star effect. A rubber band holds the construction in shape. When flattened, the band stretches. If the pressure on the flat card is released, the band contracts and the card springs dramatically into shape.*

HIDDEN JUNGLE

height 10 cm (4 in)

RIGHT *The continuous zig-zag of card (cardboard), containing the "hidden" jungle inside, is made using the Trellis technique. The zig-zag collapses and folds flat against the hard surfaces at the back of the photograph. These surfaces are book covers, which can close around the pop-up to create a conventional-looking, closed book.*

YA BOO SUCKS!

height 23 cm (9 in)

BELOW *This highly illustrated construction is made almost entirely from one sheet of card (cardboard) – even the tongue is integral. The only additions are the eyes and the supports behind them, which use Scenery Flats technique.*

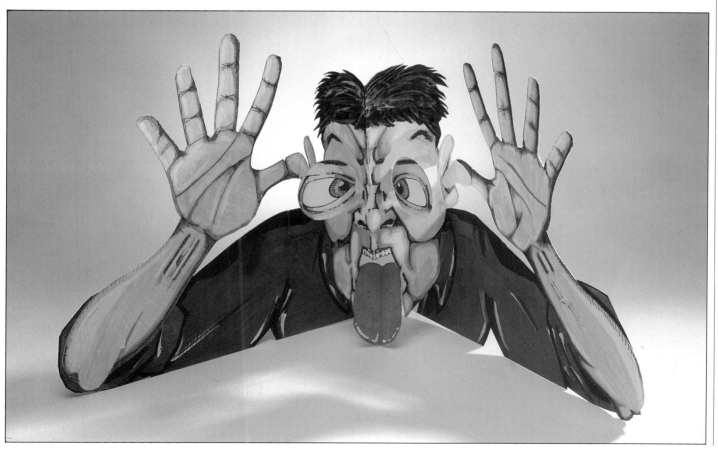

RABBIT

height 8 cm (3 in)

LEFT *A rabbit is an appropriate subject for a magician's business card. The rabbit is made here from one piece of card (cardboard), which has been cut and then folded into its final shape using simple origami techniques, then positioned astride the gutter crease.*

ABC

height 11 cm (4¼ in)

BELOW *The Steps technique is used here to great effect to describe the outline of straight and curved letter forms. In fact, the outline of any shape can be depicted in this way, and successive generations can create extra layers in front of the original one.*

HOUSE BY O.M. UNGERS
height 8 cm (3 in)

ABOVE *The basic Diagonal Box technique creates the simple box shape of the house. The separate roof, however, is created by an ingenious mechanism which swivels it into place and which is beautiful to watch as the card is opened.*

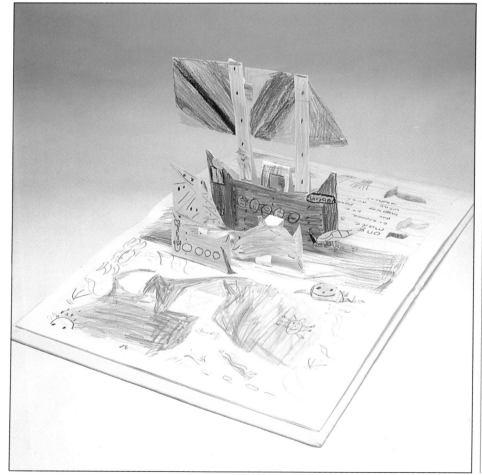

SPREAD FROM "POP-UP JOURNEY"
height 22 cm (8½ in)

RIGHT *This story-book features pop-ups designed and made by eight-year-old school children. There are several spreads, each containing a different pop-up design.*

STEAM ENGINE
height 20 cm (8¾ in)

LEFT *Built on a floating layer of the word "train", this solid-looking construction uses Box techniques to create the engine itself. The octagonal front to the boiler is particularly ingenious, closing like the iris of a camera as the backing sheet is pulled open. It is constructed from coloured card (cardboard) and decorated with gouache.*

DIGGER
height 23 cm (9 in)

BELOW *The body of the vehicle below the cab is a basic box with a rubber band stretched taut across a diagonal. When the box is pushed flat, the rubber band stretches further. Releasing the pressure on the collapsed box, allows the band to contract and erect the vehicle. In turn, this automatically erects the scoop and digger arms, fore and aft. By pulling the exhaust pipe on the bonnet, the bucket can be made to move, and by pulling the orange light on top of the cab, the digger can also be made to move!*

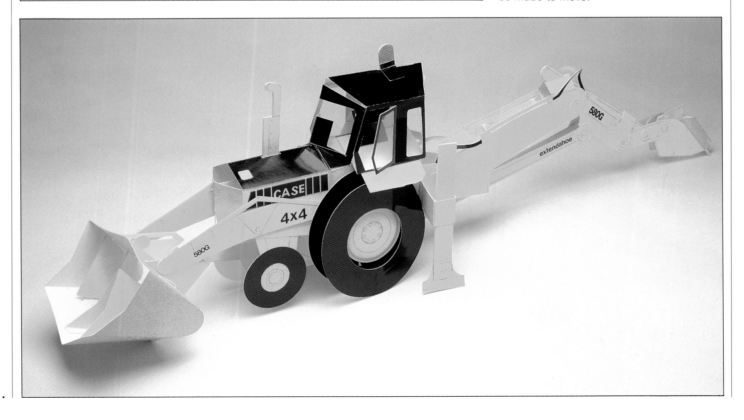

HOUSE

height 12 cm (4¾ in)

RIGHT *Designed as a promotional item, the house is a basic square-on box with simple additions. The design folds flat for mailing. When removed from its envelope, a powerful rubber band, which was stretched taut, begins to contract and automatically erects the house with great speed, and dramatic effect!*

DIGGER

height 21 cm (8¼ in)

BELOW *Stretched diagonally across the inside of the digger, a taut rubber band keeps the pop-up in shape. The construction can be pushed flat, further stretching the band. When the pressure is removed, the digger automatically pops into its three-dimensional shape!*

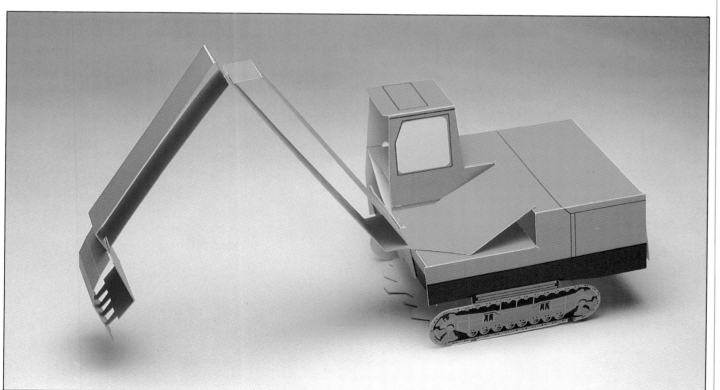

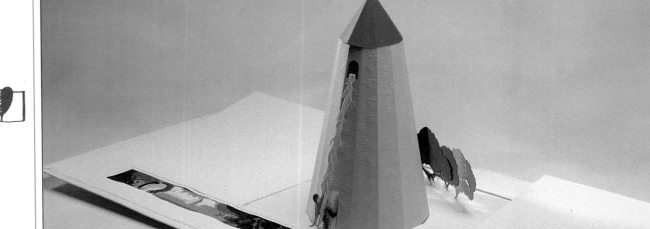

RAPUNZEL
height 28 cm (11 in)

ABOVE *The tower and its conical roof are made using the Box technique, but it has many sides instead of the more usual four or six. The large, curved, blank sheets to each side of the tower are designed to contain the text of the story. Note how the top edges lift slightly for easy reading; this is achieved by an ingenious strap system, which lifts as the spread opens.*

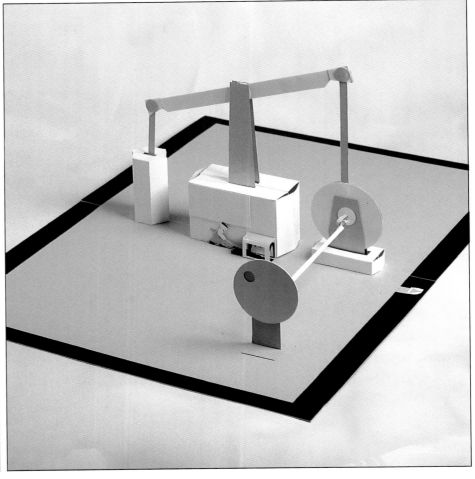

BEAM ENGINE
height 30 cm (12 in)

LEFT *The beam actually works! The grey disk in the foreground can be rotated by placing a finger on the dark spot. By a series of ingenious couplings, this drives the shaft connecting the disk to the right-hand gutter crease pop-up, which in turn rotates the white disk to operate the beam. Each of the three pop-ups along the gutter uses the Square-on Box technique. Pulling the tab on the perimeter of the backing sheet, causes the boilerman to stoke the fire.*

STORK

height 14 cm (5½ in)

RIGHT *The use of bent wire to create the legs and feet gives this design a lightness that card (cardboard) could not achieve. Although card is the natural medium for a pop-up, there is no technical reason why other materials, such as wire, cotton thread or acetate, could not also be used.*

PIRATES

height 6 cm (2¾ in)

BELOW *The shape of the rowing boat is achieved using the Square-on Box technique. The men are attached to the inside of the boat and also to a long horizontal shaft that runs through their bodies, over the gutter crease, and out at the stern. By pulling and pushing the shaft, the figures flip forwards and backwards, rowing the boat! The decoration was applied using pastel on coloured papers.*

CAPE JASMINE

height 4 cm (1½ in)

LEFT *The six petals pop up and fold flat in the form of a horizontal box, though here the panels are splayed almost to the horizontal. The central structure is slotted together in the same way as the Tulip (page 84).*

TWO BUDDHAS

height 15 cm (6 in) and 11 cm (4¾ in)

BELOW *These two commercially available cards are part of a larger series of Buddhas, all made as one-piece pop-ups. They make intricate use of the Generations and Cut Away techniques. Note that, unusually, the only straight edges occur in the short horizontal creases. Also note that all the cut edges are curved.*

COW

height 8 cm (3 in)

RIGHT *This simple pop-up makes good use of the upturned Horizontal "V" technique. The udder hangs from the crease along the spine. Many animals can be made using this folded spine technique. The card is decorated with marker pens.*

FANTASY BIRD

height 32 cm (12½ in)

BELOW *This complex, but symmetrical construction is made using a combination of Box and Floating Layers techniques. Interestingly, it is not astride the gutter crease, but sits to one side at the end of a strap. This off-centre placement makes the construction appear less symmetrical and less static.*

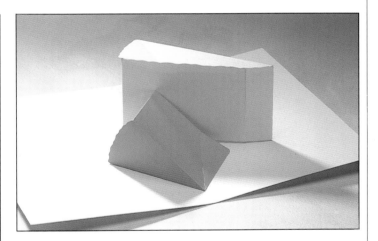

CHEESES

height 8 cm (3 in)

ABOVE *Although the forms are simple, this design was constructed with great technical skill. Both wedges of cheese are solid, not open at the back, and made using a combination of Box techniques and Horizontal "V" techniques, filled in across the top. The result is a design which looks unusually solid and asymmetric.*

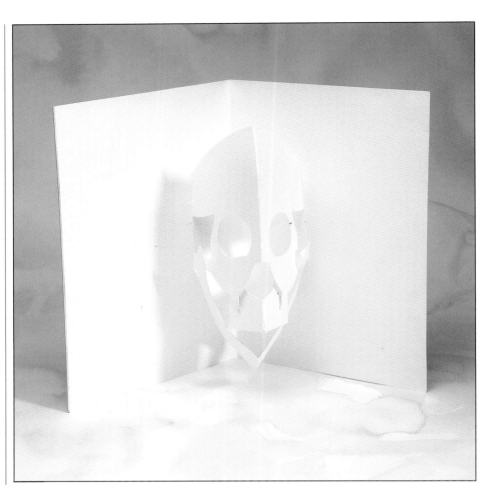

WASP AND BUG
height 33 cm (13 in)

OPPOSITE TOP *This exquisite construction pops up using a technique similar to exercise I of the Pivot technique. Note the way in which the different media are used, in particular the use of dried leaves, the delicate cutting of strands of card (cardboard) to the left of the design, the beautiful detailed painting of the insects, and the use of acetate and wire to form the wasp's wings. For a pop-up, this design was made in an unusually poetic manner.*

SKULL
height 30 cm (12 in)

LEFT *This three-piece design makes use of the upturned Horizontal "V" technique, to create a convincing representation of a skull. By being thrust forward from the gutter crease, a sense of volume is created.*

THREE ABSTRACTS
height 25 cm (9¾ in)

BELOW *These beautiful, intricate one-piece designs are part of a long series of abstracts by the same designer. They make complex use of the Generations and Steps techniques, but also use light and shade in a positive way to achieve their dazzling and dramatic effects.*

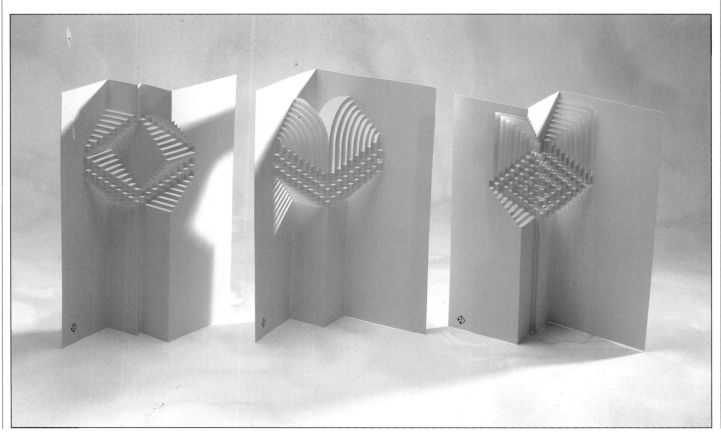

GORILLAS
height
30 cm (12 in)
RIGHT *In this eccentric and humorous design (made all the more humorous when the banana is seen moving) the fruit itself is constructed using nothing more than the basic example from the Single Slit Angle of Crease technique – the very first pop-up technique in the book. The shape of the slit is made more complex though, to create the shape of the banana.*

MEILLEURS VOEUX POUR 1992
height 15 cm (6 in)
BELOW *Produced for a French company as a New Year card for its clients, this one-piece pop-up makes unusual use of the Steps technique. The steps are not cut square, but at a shallow angle, to create an intriguing visual effect. Note how the card is a double layer at the back. The platform at the top of the steps slots into the back layer, locking the construction.*

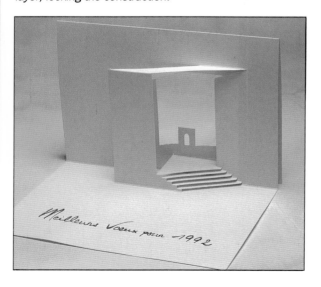

THE POP-UP COOKOUT COOKBOOK

LEFT height 37 cm (14½ in)
When fully opened, the different pop-up friezes extended to a width of 150 cm (60 in). The piece was made specifically for an exhibition organized around the theme of a barbecue. The quality of the decoration, in particular the cheeky use of the dishcloth fabric, gives interest to a simple pop-up technique.

RHYTHMIC NOTES OF SEVEN FOLDS

height 22 cm (8½ in)
BELOW *Using spray paint on paper printing plates, the designer was able to create spontaneous effects in offset printing, which usually requires several intermediate steps before a final image can be created. The result adds textural interest to a one-piece pop-up which, when the zig-zag pleats are unfolded, extends to a length of 150 cm (60 in).*

Index

Acknowledgements

I would like to thank students from the following design courses for their invaluable contributions to the book: students from the Foundation Graphics course, Ravensbourne College of Design and Communication, for creating many of the Techniques pop-ups; students from the BA Hons Graphic Information Design course, Westminster University and from the HND Graphic Design course, Amersham and Wycombe College, for making many of the Heart pop-ups.

I would also like to thank Bärbel Speck-Schifferer for her research and Tim Rowett for the loan of pop-ups from his collection.

Finally, I must thank the many pop-up devotees – amateur and professional – without whose enthusiastic support this book could not have been written.

The papers and cards used to construct the Techniques exercises were kindly supplied by G.F. Smith and Son of Hull and London (tel: 0482-23503; fax: 0482-223174).

Design

Page 8, Domberger KG, 70794 Filderstadt, Germany; page 21, Arthur Day; page 25, William Lewis; page 27, Kevin Perry/3rd Dimension; page 30, Justin Zillies; page 42, Louise Webb; page 45, Jennifer Vaughn; page 47, Brigite Knoblauh; page 50, Denise James; page 56, Masahiro Chatani; page 59, Michele Testa; page 61, Masahiro Chatani; page 65, Eberhard Dorschfeldt; page 67, Sara Thompson; page 68, David Swift; page 71, Jane Shearman; page 76, Neil Scoggins; page 79, Melissa Downs; page 84, Keiko Nakazawa; page 86, Robert Evans; page 89, Isabelle Martin; page 91, Paul Austin; page 92, Debbie Atkins; page 96, Paul Johnson; page 103, Rachel Parfitt; page 107, Colin Hewitt; page 111, Neil Horne; page 113, Darryl Moulton; page 119, Adam Freakley; page 123, David Malarkey; page 129, Hartmut Rädar/ Wohnzubehör Gmblt, 4630 Bochum, Germany; page 133, Tamsin Hamilton; page 139, Ruth Brocklehurst; page 140, Karen Sawyer; page 141, (above) Keiko Nakazawa and (below) David Malarkey; page 142, (above) Tristan Dellaway and (below) Kirsty Gwilliam; page 143, (above) Pat Phillips and (below) Jenny Tillotson; page 144, Masahiro Chatani; page 145, (top) Keiko Nakazawa, (below right) Lyn Hourahine/Paper Power and (below left) David Malarkey; page 146, (above) Tracy James and (below) Lyn Hourahine/ Paper Power; page 147, (above) Pat Phillips and (below) Stephan Dilkes; page 148, (above) Arthur Day and (below) Hartmut Rädar/ Wohnzubehör Gmblt, 4630 Bochum, Germany; page 149, (above) Hartmut Radar and (below) classroom project led by Paul Johnson; page 150, (above) Daniel Holden and (below) Roger Hardy; page 151, (above) Kevin Perry/Kee Scott for Sun Alliance and (below) Roger Hardy; page 152, (above) Geoff Rayner and (below) Paul Dunning; page 153; (above) David Malarkey and (below) Ayaz Gité; page 154, Keiko Nakazawa; page 155, (top and bottom right) David Malarkey and (bottom left) Paul Johnson; page 156, (above) Christine Brazel and (below) Eberhard Dorschfeldt; page 157, (top) David Swift, (bottom left) Mikael Mourgue-Sanders and (bottom) Didier Boursin; and page 158, Carol Barton. All the remaining uncredited pop-ups were made by the author.

The Author

Paul Jackson is a professional paper-engineer and paper artist, who has designed pop-ups and paper models for a wide range of corporate clients. In addition, he has written several acclaimed papercraft books and has lectured extensively in the United Kingdom, Germany and the USA, to students of Art and Design. His own paper works have been exhibited in Europe, the America and Japan. He has demonstrated his skills on television many times.